Recovering Consolation

"Greg Maillet has provided a thorough examination of Tolkien's Catholic worldview as it shapes his writing. In his focus on Sam Gamgee as an example of humble Christian discipleship, Maillet gives us a touchstone; this is a fresh and deeply informed perspective on the greatest modern epic in Western literature which helps explain how, even for non-Christian readers, Tolkien's fiction has successfully communicated a sense of abiding truth, and withal, deep consolation."

—**David Lyle Jeffrey,**
resident distinguished professor,
Baylor Institute for Studies in Religion, Baylor University

"In exalting Sam Gamgee as the true hero of *The Lord of the Rings*—after all, Frodo finally fails to destroy the Sauronic Ring of coercive power—Greg Maillet has produced a refreshing new study of what may one day be regarded as the twentieth century's most important book. It is no small praise to say of *Recovering Consolation* that it should be read as it is written—devotionally."

—**Ralph C. Wood,**
professor emeritus of theology and literature,
Baylor University

"*Recovering Consolation* is not only an outstanding exegesis of Tolkien's *The Lord of the Rings*, it opens a series of portals to profound understanding of human nature, of the war between good and evil, and the mysteries of divine providence. As layer upon layer of meaning are revealed, Greg Maillet's readers will find themselves deeply moved and thrilled with unexpected illuminations. This is far more than a superb intellectual exercise; it is a beautiful integration of scholarship with holy wisdom."

—**Michael David O'Brien,**
author of *Island of the World*

"Who's the true hero of *The Lord of the Rings*? Is it Frodo? Or Gandalf? Or possibly Aragorn? According to Tolkien, it was none of these. The true hero of *The Lord of the Rings* was none other than Samwise Gamgee. This is Tolkien's view, and it is the view of Greg Maillet, author of this wonderful book. Thanks to Maillet's fine scholarship and deep knowledge of Tolkien's epic, we can now follow the footsteps of Sam, the least likely of heroes, and discover why the humble are worth exalting."

—**Joseph Pearce,**
author of *Tolkien: Man and Myth*

"Greg Maillet makes a compelling case that Sam Gamgee embodies the ennoblement of humility at the center of Tolkien's artistic vision. By combining historical and literary learning with theological insight, this study reveals the integral role of the affections and the imagination in the growth of faith, hope, and love. Whether discussing how mortals face death or the history of the word 'caution,' Maillet models a tact of heart and mind that Tolkien's writing deserves."

—**Phillip J. Donnelly,**
professor of literature, Baylor University

"Many of Tolkien's readers consider Samwise Gamgee the hero of Tolkien's *Lord of the Rings*. In this first book-length study of Sam, Greg Maillet takes us deep into this character's soul. From Sam's humble origins to the end of his remarkable adventures, Maillet is a sure guide to what makes this character so beloved. Consolation truly awaits those who revisit with Maillet both the perils and the beauties that this hardy Hobbit encounters as he finds his way into one of those 'stories that really matter.'"

—**Thomas L. Martin,**
professor of English, Wheaton College

Recovering Consolation

Sam's Enchanted Path in *The Lord of the Rings*

GREG MAILLET

PICKWICK Publications · Eugene, Oregon

RECOVERING CONSOLATION
Sam's Enchanted Path in *The Lord of the Rings*

Copyright © 2024 Greg Maillet. All rights reserved. Except for brief quotations in critical publications or reviews, no part of this book may be reproduced in any manner without prior written permission from the publisher. Write: Permissions, Wipf and Stock Publishers, 199 W. 8th Ave., Suite 3, Eugene, OR 97401.

Pickwick Publications
An Imprint of Wipf and Stock Publishers
199 W. 8th Ave., Suite 3
Eugene, OR 97401

www.wipfandstock.com

PAPERBACK ISBN: 978-1-6667-8514-2
HARDCOVER ISBN: 978-1-6667-8515-9
EBOOK ISBN: 978-1-6667-8516-6

Cataloguing-in-Publication data:

Names: Maillet, Greg [author].

Title: Recovering consolation : Sam's enchanted path in *The Lord of the Rings* / Greg Maillet.

Description: Eugene, OR: Pickwick Publications, 2024 | Includes bibliographical references.

Identifiers: ISBN 978-1-6667-8514-2 (paperback) | ISBN 978-1-6667-8515-9 (hardcover) | ISBN 978-1-6667-8516-6 (ebook)

Subjects: LCSH: Tolkien, J. R. R. (John Ronald Reuel), 1892–1973. Lord of the rings. | Gamgee, Samwise—Fiction. | Tolkien, J. R. R. (John Ronald Reuel), 1892–1973. | Middle Earth (Imaginary place). | Myth in literature. | Fantasy fiction, English.

Classification: PR6039.O32 M35 2024 (paperback) | PR6039.O32 (ebook)

VERSION NUMBER 11/08/24

All material from *The Lord of the Rings* reprinted by permission of HarperCollins Publishers Ltd.

For my children: Jenelle, Samuel, and Madeleine.

If you wish to understand our times, you should read *The Lord of the Rings*. It is the greatest myth of our age. It tells of the war in heavens come down to earth, and thus as the reader lives inside the story, he returns to our own war with fresh eyes and better understanding.

MICHAEL D. O'BRIEN, *THE SABBATICAL*[1]

I think the simple "rustic" love of Sam and his Rosie (nowhere elaborated) is absolutely essential to the study of his (the chief hero's) character, and to the theme of the relation of ordinary life (breathing, eating, working, begetting) and quests, sacrifice, causes and the "longing for Elves," and sheer beauty.

J. R. R. TOLKIEN, "LETTER 131"[2]

What we call the didactic is often the enchanted.

C. S. LEWIS, *A PREFACE TO PARADISE LOST*[3]

---

1. O'Brien, *Sabbatical*, 186.
2. Tolkien, *Letters*, 229.
3. Lewis, *Preface*.

Contents

*Introduction: Tolkien and Catholicism, or,
Eucatastrophe and the Eucharist* | 1

BOOK ONE | 13

1. A Long-Expected Party: "Everyone's Invited" | 13
2. The Shadow of the Past:
   "Who Invented the Stories Anyway?" | 16
3. Three Is Company: "Elves, Sir!" | 21
4. "A Short-Cut to Mushrooms": "I Must See It Through" | 24
5. A Conspiracy Unmasked: "We Are Your Friends" | 26
6. The Old Forest: "There's More behind
   This than Sun and Warm Air" | 28
7. In the House of Tom Bombadil: "Moonlight
   and Starlight and the Wind off the Hilltop" | 30
8. Fog on the Barrow-Downs: "Where Are My Clothes?" | 33
9. At the Sign of the Prancing Pony: "We Surely Aren't
   Going to Stay Here for the Night, Are We Sir?" | 36
10. Strider: "I Never Heard No Good of Such Folk" | 38
11. A Knife in the Dark: "I Would Like to Hear More
    about Elves; The Dark Seems to Press Round So Close" | 41
12. Flight to the Ford: "What Is
    the Matter with My Master?" | 43

BOOK TWO | 46

1. Many Meetings: "Glory and Trumpets" | 46
2. The Council of Elrond: "A Nice Pickle" | 49
3. The Ring Goes South: "If You Don't Let Me Go With You, Sam, I'll Follow on My Own" | 53
4. A Journey in the Dark: "My Heart's Right Down in My Toes" | 55
5. The Bridge of Khazad-Dûm: "Weeping" | 58
6. Lothlórien: "Inside a Song" | 60
7. The Mirror of Galadriel: "I Saw a Star" | 64
8. Farewell to Lórien: "Something Inaudible" | 67
9. The Great River: "I Saw a Log with Eyes!" | 69
10. The Breaking of the Fellowship: "Think, If You Can!" | 72

BOOK FOUR | 76

A Eucatastrophic Plot Turn | 76

1. The Taming of Sméagol: "We're in a Fix, and No Mistake" | 78
2. The Passage of the Marshes: "Where's That Dratted Creature?" | 82
3. The Black Gate Is Closed: "Beyond Any Gamgee to Guess" | 84
4. Of Herbs and Stewed Rabbit: "What a Life!" | 87
5. The Window on the West: "That Was Good and True" | 90
6. The Forbidden Pool: "Chilly to the Heart" | 93
7. Journey to the Cross-Roads: "Where There's Life There's Hope" | 95
8. The Stairs of Cirith Ungol: "The Tales That Really Mattered" | 96

9. Shelob's Lair: "The Lady's Gift!" | 99

10. The Choices of Master Samwise: "May I Be Forgiven!" | 102

Interlude | 105

BOOK SIX | 107

1. The Tower of Cirith Ungol:
"Above All Shadows Rides the Sun" | 107

2. The Land of Shadow:
"All We Want Is Light and Water" | 109

3. Mount Doom: "No Words" | 113

4. The Field of Cormallen: "Like Spring After Winter" | 117

5. The Steward and the King: "I Would Dearly Love
to See Bywater Again, and Rosie Cotton and Her Brothers,
and the Gaffer and Marigold and All" | 120

6. Many Partings: "I Wish I Was Going Back to Lórien!" | 121

7. Homeward Bound: "Another Wish Come True" | 123

8. The Scouring of the Shire: "It Is Home" | 124

9. The Grey Havens: "Well, I'm Back" | 128

Conclusion | 131

A Sanctified Hobbit-Hero | 131

Bibliography | 139

Introduction
Tolkien and Catholicism, or,
Eucatastrophe and the Eucharist

Seek the consolation of the ages at the end of a star trail.
Thomas L. Martin, Christ the Life[1]

This is a small book about a small person, and dedicated to small people everywhere. Yet I remain convinced that its topic is important. By our time in the twenty-first century, *The Lord of the Rings* is firmly established as one of the great novels in world literature and as one of the greatest Catholic novels ever written. A large group of the best theological minds of our time, many of whom appear in my bibliography, have helped to firmly establish the latter claim. In particular, three critics have aided my walk with Sam: Fleming Rutledge, Ralph Wood, and Craig Bernthal.[2] It is no accident, perhaps, that this trinity represents three distinct forms of Christianity to whom Tolkien seems especially relevant: Anglican, Baptist, and Roman Catholic. My own bias is to the latter, but very much affirm Bernthal's succinct point: great Catholic writers assert a "Christian reality" because they simply believe that it is "reality."[3]

All Christian readers of Tolkien are aided very much by an oft-quoted letter that Tolkien wrote to Robert Murray, SJ, the priest who gave his

---

1. Martin, *Christ the Life*, 6.

2. See Rutledge, *Battle for Middle-earth*; Wood, *Gospel According to Tolkien*; and Bernthal, *Tolkien's Sacramental Vision*.

3. Bernthal, *Sacramental*, 6.

funeral. Murray had found in *The Lord of the Rings* a "positive compatibility with the order of grace,"[4] and was particularly reminded of Mary by Galadriel, the elf-queen. Tolkien replied that "of course" his novel is "fundamentally Catholic"; this letter goes on to describe Catholicism as "a Faith that has nourished me and taught me all the little I know," and fondly recalls his mother, "who clung to her conversion and died young, largely through the hardships of poverty resulting from it."[5] Tolkien's reply further affirms Murray likening Galadriel to "Our Lady, upon which all my small perception of beauty both in majesty and simplicity is founded."[6] Yet in the same letter, Tolkien further claims that his revision of the novel has "cut out practically all references to anything like 'religion.'"[7] The paradoxical question, then, is how did this revision make the novel more Catholic?

Eminent scholar Tom Shippey is probably correct that part of the novel's broad appeal is a world without public revelation,[8] but the more well-known objection to a religious interpretation of Tolkien derives from the author's own words. Equally oft-quoted as the letter to Murray is the second foreword that Tolkien added to the second edition of his novel, in 1966; whereas the first preface of the novel focused on fascinating topics such as the sources of Shire tobacco or how Gollum first got the ring, the second has this critical idea:

> I cordially dislike allegory in all its manifestations, and always have done so since I grew old and wary enough to detect its presence. I much prefer history, true or feigned, with its varied applicability to the thought and experience of readers. I think that many confuse "applicability" and "allegory"; but one resides in the freedom of the reader, and the other in the purposed domination of the author.[9]

Further comparison, for example, of Galadriel to Mary is typically dismissed as "allegory," and legions of Tolkien fans (especially on the internet) explore Tolkien's work without any reference to religion at all.

For at least two reasons, however, one can view this current of affairs as another example of one of Tolkien's major themes: good coming out of evil. First, while it does not seem good to use Tolkien's work as simply an

---

4. Tolkien, *Letters*, 257.
5. Tolkien, *Letters*, 257–58.
6. Tolkien, *Letter*, 257.
7. Tolkien, *Letters*, 257.
8. Shippey, *Author of the Century*, 175–82.
9. Tolkien, *Lord of the Rings*, xxiv.

escape from reality, and Tolkien's other letters insist that "Middle-earth is not an imaginary world"[10] and draw many connections to our faith, Catholics should be the first to reject simple allegorical readings. For *of course* Mary herself is far greater than any fictional character, and *of course* a devout Catholic, as Tolkien's biography shows him to be, would never propose any literature text as a substitute for divine revelation. As Tolkien puts it in another letter, "The Incarnation of God is an *infinitely* greater thing than anything I would dare to write."[11] This is not false humility, but a statement of obvious fact to anyone who believes in the existence of God and the truth of Christian revelation.

Secondly, even abjuring simple allegory, one might be tempted to "typology," the form of allegory which acknowledges historical differences between key figures, but finds the great significance of one in how it points to Christian revelation, as for example how Joseph in *Genesis* points to Jesus. Though less obviously problematic than allegory, an exclusive typological reading minimizes the extensive background of Tolkien's characters; the multi-dimensional quality of Tolkien's legendarium is an important element of its depth. Devoted fans of Tolkien's first and second ages (through posthumous texts edited by Tolkien's son, Christopher, such as *The Silmarillion* and *The History of Middle-earth*), give often fascinating details that help us understand the "third age" presented in *The Lord of the Rings*. Moreover, Tolkien's legendarium cannot point to Christ with the divinely intended form of the Old Testament, for its author is human not divine. So neither allegory nor typology are open as means of theological aesthetics helpful to understanding Tolkien. But then how can one validly apply Catholicism to Tolkien's work, as he himself does so often in other letters?

My main answer to this crucial question is Samwise Gamgee, whom Tolkien's letters call "this jewel among the hobbits"[12] and "the chief hero"[13] of the novel. Such high praise is strictly external, however, for within the novel's pages Sam is a model of humble service to his master Frodo. Yet it is precisely because Sam is the "ultimate servant" that he becomes the "ultimate hero."[14] Rutledge makes a similar claim, calling Sam "the model

---

10. Tolkien, *Letters*, 345.
11. Tolkien, *Letters*, 343.
12. Tolkien, *Letters*, 126.
13. Tolkien, *Letters*, 229.
14. Wood, *Gospel*, 164.

of the true Christian disciple,"[15] but to properly understand the leading role that Tolkien gives Sam, one must also be fairly familiar with the ideas of "On Fairy-Stories," a lecture printed before and after his epic novel.[16] This lecture, in my opinion, does more than any other critical account to explain the "faërie" genre that Tolkien's literary art practices.

"On Fairy-Stories" mainly seeks to clarify the genre in which Tolkien writes. "Faërie" itself is not mainly concerned with stories about the tiny, winged creatures of popular myth, but rather "the realm or state in which faëries have their being." It includes many things generally regarded as fictional, including "witches, trolls, giants, or dragons." Moderns generally term this realm "magic," but Tolkien clarifies that "it is magic of a peculiar mood and power, at the furthest pole from the vulgar devices of the laborious, scientific magician." It is a magic that does not deceive, but rather recovers concrete reality: "the sun, the moon, the sky; and the earth, and all things that are in it: tree and bird, water and stone, wine and bread, and ourselves, mortal men, when we are enchanted."

"Enchantment" and "recovery" are thus key terms within the genre, though adults often take this less seriously than the fascination children often have for such stories. "Is it true?" the naïve question of children, remains an important, valid question, for the "magic of Faërie" often considers "primordial human desires." While certainly offering "escape" from morbid material reality, the "recovery" offered by fairy-stories also points towards "consolation." "It was in fairy-stories," Tolkien affirms, that "I first divined the potency of words, and the wonder of the things, such as stone, and wood, and iron; tree and grass; house and fire; bread and wine."[17]

The diction here suggests already the connection that Tolkien sees between natural, concrete reality and supernatural Catholic doctrine, but this is affirmed much more explicitly in the lecture's epilogue. First Tolkien makes clear that "the consolation of fairy-stories has another aspect than the imaginative satisfaction of ancient desires," an aspect that Tolkien calls "eucatastrophe" to contrast the "happy endings" of fairy stories with the catastrophes of history. He further defines "eucatastrophe" as a "sudden turn to joy," which "denies (in the face of much evidence, if you will) universal final defeat and in so far is *evangelium*, giving a fleeting glimpse of Joy, Joy beyond the walls of this world, poignant as grief." The epilogue then makes

15. Rutledge, *Battle for Middle-earth*, 203.
16. See Tolkien, "On Fairy-Stories."
17. Tolkien, "On Fairy-Stories," 60.

INTRODUCTION

clear that while the child's valid question—"is it true?"—can be answered in strictly aesthetic terms, via the inner consistency of the imagined world, "eucatastrophe" can also be "a far-off gleam or echo of *evangelium* in the real world." Applicable to Christian understanding of the ancient word for the Christian gospel, the applicability of "eucatastrophe" to the most concrete Catholic expression of this gospel, the Eucharist, is then spelled out by Tolkien in the most explicit doctrinal terms:

> The Birth of Christ is the *eucatastrophe* of Man's history. The Resurrection is the *eucatastrophe* of the story of the Incarnation. This story begins and ends in joy.... This story is supreme, and it is true. Art has been verified. God is the Lord, of angels, and of men—and of Elves. Legend and History have met and fused. But... the Evangelium has not abrogated legends, it has hallowed them, especially the "happy ending."[18]

A coined word, "eucatastrophe" is clearly related to "eucharist," which etymologically suggests "thanks for the goodness" of God's grace. However, as the central sacrament of Catholic doctrine, dogmatically defined by the term "trans-substantiation," commonly known as the "summit and summary of the faith," "eucharist" clearly means much more. We have ample evidence that Tolkien affirmed Jesus's radical claim that "He that eateth my flesh and drinketh my blood hath eternal life" (John 6:54), arguing that "we must therefore either believe in Him and in what he said and take the consequences; or reject him and take the consequences."[19] Perhaps most movingly, Tolkien tells his son Michael:

> I set before you the one great thing to love on earth: the Blessed Sacrament.... There you will find romance, glory, honor, fidelity, and the true way of all your loves upon earth, and more than that: Death: by the divine paradox, that which ends life, and demands the surrender of all, and yet by the taste (or foretaste) of which alone can what you seek in your earthly relationships (love, faithfulness, joy) be maintained, or take on that complexion of reality, of eternal endurance, which every man's heart desires.[20]

Many quote only the pleasant opening lines here, but I include the "divine paradox" for a specific reason: Catholicism impacts Tolkien's art in a very existential way, grounded in the age that formed him, Newman's nineteenth

18. Tolkien, "On Fairy-Stories," 72–73.
19. Tolkien, *Letters*, 475.
20. Tolkien, *Letters*, 74.

century, and continued to inspire him throughout his life. From our distant vantage point in the twenty-first century, even if we ourselves are Catholic, it is quite possible to miss the connection that Tolkien's faith, and fiction, makes between the eucharist, eucatastrophe, and a sacrifice that leads both to physical death and spiritual joy. The Catholic sacraments, especially baptism and the eucharist, clearly remind us, as Bernthal frequently notes, that death, temporally, is "the last enemy" to be "destroyed" (1 Cor 15:26). In *The Silmarillion*, however, Tolkien is orthodox in terming death "the gift of Ilúvatar," upon which Melkor "has cast his shadow," in order to bring "forth evil out of good, and fear out of hope."[21] Catholicism, and Tolkien, frequently show the opposite—God bringing good out of evil and thus sustaining hope even in our darkest days. Even Melkor's rebellion is turned to good by God, and becomes merely "a tributary" of God's "glory."[22]

Holly Ordway has invaluably shown that Tolkien was often modern rather than medieval in his reading,[23] and was especially influenced by Newman's Oratorian Order, especially, of course, Father Francis Morgan who raised Tolkien and his brother Hilary after they were orphaned. Yet Tolkien was a far too learned medievalist not to bring more from that world into his fiction likely to ever be perceived by moderns. One common practice of Catholic art that seems obvious in Tolkien is the tracing of the Triune Creator in Creation, which St. Augustine famously describes in *De Trinitate*, and which Latinists of the later Middle Ages commonly commend as *forma tractatus*; Dante's *terza rima* is likely the most famous example of this,[24] but it is a commonplace, to quote one manual of the period: "Because of the Trinity, because a triple cord is hard to break, because St. Bernard's sermons had three points, and because three points take up about the right amount of time."[25] Tolkien's fiction is art, of course, not homiletics, but the ethical aesthetic essential to medieval art often recurs in Tolkien. Literary order often mirrors the Order of the Universe, hence it is important to consider *The Lord of the Rings* chronologically, a point that Rutledge stresses as a "narrative strategy."[26]

21. Tolkien, *Silmarillion*, 29–30.
22. Tolkien, *Silmarillion*, 5.
23. Ordway, *Tolkien's Modern Reading*.
24. Another famous example is Rublev's painting *The Holy Trinity*, depicting the visitors to Abraham at Mamre.
25. Translation in Allen, *Ethical Poetic*, 27.
26. Rutledge, *Battle*, 1–4.

Introduction

The clarity and precision of Tolkien's own developed thought on the theological aesthetic of his work, "On Fairy-Stories," especially its epilogue, bears much commentary, medieval and modern, but for my purposes here let it simply suffice to confirm its applicability to Tolkien's legendarium as a whole. Sam consistently shows a strong imaginative interest in faërie, but also a concern with concrete, practical matters not typically associated with theology. He is plain-speaking, and if we are not listening closely to his words we can easily miss their important link to Tolkien's most profound thoughts. Sam is particularly familiar, for example, with the ancient legends that often become present rather than past in crucial characters and events in *The Lord of the Rings*. Characters such as Elrond or Galadriel were alive in the earlier age, and their personal histories do matter in the conflicts depicted by the later fiction.

This fact is perhaps most relevant in the conflict of Gandalf and Sauron, chief spiritual combatants in the third age but alive since the first as servants to opposites: Gandalf serves the "Ainur" loyal to Ilúvatar, the deity who creates Middle-earth, while Sauron is servant to Melkor, the rebel Ainur who becomes an enemy to God much as Lucifer becomes Satan in the Bible. Tolkien's letters explicitly liken Satan's fall to how, in his "myth Morgoth"—whom the fallen Melkor becomes—"fell before Creation of the physical world."[27] As most literary critics and theologians would recognize, Melkor is "like Satan in Milton's epic."[28] This "allegory" is not exact, but certainly "applicable" enough to set up the "spiritual warfare" motif that runs throughout *The Lord of the Rings*.

As already noted, Tolkien typically makes religion implicit rather than explicit within his work. Within his novel, Tolkien's letters affirm, "there is no embodiment of the One, of God," but "the One retains all ultimate authority, and (or so it seems as viewed in serial time) reserves the right to intrude the finger of God into the story."[29] Perhaps Tolkien's central term for God is "the Writer of the Story (by which I do not mean myself); 'that one ever-present Person who is never absent and never named' (as one critic has said)."[30] This metaphor explicitly raises the central issue related to God's role in history, the familiar but complex theological question of the

---

27. Tolkien, *Letters*, 350.
28. Wood, *Gospel*, 50.
29. Tolkien, *Letters*, 341.
30. Tolkien, *Letters*, 363.

relation between fate, predestination, free will, and providence.[31] As Frodo asks in a key passage we will come to, is "the story already written"? Above all other themes, another letter states definitively, the novel "is about God, and His sole right to divine honor."[32]

Sauron is Lord of the "one ring" of power in this world, as Satan is "Prince of this World," but by novel's end we can see that God alone is the one Lord of all the rings. "Tolkien's world," as Wood puts it, is "thoroughly theocentric," "inescapably God-centered."[33] Elvish linguists can tell us, and Tolkien confirms,[34] that the full name of deity in Middle-earth, "*Eru Ilúvatar*" means "the One Father of All'"; yet it is surely also an application of biblical conceptions of the divine being "the light of the world," as "God" is an Anglo-Saxon rendering of the "Good." Of course, it is not an allegorical synonym for the Triune God whom Christianity must affirm. There is another element of Tolkien's creation myth, the "Ainulindalë" (usually printed at the start of *The Silmarillion*), which is even more applicable to Catholic Theology. For Tolkien does not present Melkor and Ilúvatar as equal opposites; rather, as with God and the rebel Angels in the Bible, as for example when Satan enters Judas just before Christ's passion (Luke 22:3; John 13:27), God actually uses the very means by which evil attacks the good to bring about something new and even better than before. For Tolkien, Melkor plays a music that he takes to be his own, rebellious strains against God, but Tolkien's God does not simply destroy "the discord of Melkor"; rather, Melkor's "most triumphant notes were taken by" Ilúvatar and "woven into its own solemn pattern," Ilúvatar says to Melkor:

> And thou, Melkor, shalt see that no theme may be played that hath not its uttermost source in me, nor can any alter the music in my despite. For he that attempteth this shall prove but mine instrument in the devising of things more wonderful, which he himself hath not imagined.[35]

Throughout his legendarium, Tolkien portrays the living God as a Being who brings good out of evil in often surprising ways. To quote the words of St. Paul, "God worketh all things for the good of those who love him"

---

31. Many theologians find Tolkien's presentation of this issue profound. See Rutledge, *Battle for Middle-earth*, 110–13.
32. Tolkien, *Letters*, 350.
33. Wood, *Gospel*, 11.
34. Tolkien, *Letters*, 302.
35. Tolkien, *Silmarillion*, 5.

(Rom 8:28), though how this works for those who profess to hate God often produces what Psalm 6 calls "the mystery of iniquity." The pain and manifest agony of Christ on Calvary gives the greatest good for humanity, but what ultimately happens to Satan or Judas? Why did Jesus choose Judas as a disciple?

No author's words can be taken as the sole guide to his art, but as a starting point they are often helpful. As another Tolkien letter further explains, *The Lord of the Rings* often gives us "glimpses of a large history in the background," and this attracts us like "the towers of a distant city gleaming in a sunlit mist."[36] Yet this mythical background never overshadows or obscures the unique meaning of a specific, later story.

Allowing us both to treat the ancient legend as "background" and to savor their beauty and truth is a key part of Sam's role in *The Lord of the Rings*. Sam is also a key example of the main reason that Tolkien's fiction focuses on hobbits (as opposed to the Elves who dominate *The Silmarillion*) in the third age; in his letters, Tolkien explains that "to be hobbito-centric" means the "ennoblement (or sanctification) of the humble."[37] "Sanctification" here cannot be understood as the full path to holiness followed in Catholicism, but neither can it be entirely secularized as some synonym for "goodness." From the first time we meet Gandalf as "Olórin" early in *The Silmarillion*, his chief interest in hobbits derives from his interest in "pity and patience."[38] Sam does selflessly serve Frodo, and Sam's spirit is a key antidote to the poison of pride and power that is the essence of the ring that Frodo's quest aims to destroy. Tolkien notes that some readers are irritated by Sam's flaws,[39] but also calls him "the most closely drawn character"[40]; we learn from Sam precisely because Tolkien makes Sam "his principal hero without minimizing his limitations and defects."[41]

Adopting Sam as our main guide can seem limiting, as he appears in only four of the novel's six main books. I am forced to omit my own favorite character in the novel, Treebeard, which some students over the years have called me (not in tribute; I am tall, talk slowly, and often daydream about my wife). Each chapter title in these books of the novel become my

36. Tolkien, *Letters*, 469.
37. Tolkien, *Letters*, 343.
38. Tolkien, *Silmarillion*, 18.
39. Tolkien, *Letters*, 464.
40. Tolkien, *Letters*, 151.
41. Rutledge, *Battle*, 215.

chapters' titles, followed by words from Sam himself. In all cases except one, Sam's words are in the chapter being studied, but the more important purpose is given by Frodo in the great discourse on tales that he shares with Sam at "The Stairs of Cirith Ungol": "I want to hear more about Sam, dad. Why didn't they put in more of his talk, dad? That's what I like, it makes me laugh. And Frodo wouldn't have got far without Sam, would he, dad?" Sam humbly chides his master for "making fun," but Frodo replies that his childish voice is serious. Laughter, and children's perspectives, are taken seriously by Tolkien,[42] for Sam is much more than "semi-comic relief."[43] Hearing more of Sam's words do help us to understand the aesthetic and spiritual strengths that are gained via Tolkien's division of the fellowship. We will, for example, be able to consider carefully the final, climactic chapter of Book IV in *The Two Towers*, "The Choices of Master Samwise," one of many key elements of the novel obscured by Peter Jackson's ill-fated choice to exaggerate the importance of the battle of Helm's Deep. To his credit, Jackson's films did conclude with the same scene as Tolkien's novel, with the then married Sam returning to his beloved Rosie and welcoming their first daughter, Elanor, into his lap. As Tolkien is implying in the letter cited as an epigraph to this preface, Sam's love for Rosie is as important, to the plot and themes of the novel, as the love of Aragorn and Arwen; further, this "rustic" love is directly connected to the recovery of concrete "ordinary life," and further related to "sheer beauty." Sam's enchanted aesthetics are often Tolkien's own, and Sam's recovery of concrete reality, however much it may seem like fantasy to the unfaithful, often leads to eucatastrophic joy.

There are surely many theological topics worth focusing upon in Tolkien, but what finally convinces me that following the sanctification of Samwise Gamgee is worthwhile is another of Tolkien's letters.[44] Carol Batten-Phelps wrote Tolkien late in his life, in 1971.[45] At the time, the author was deeply concerned with the health of his wife; Tolkien wrote a reply to Batten-Phelps, but never sent it. In her letter, Batten-Phelps spoke of finding "a sanity and sanctity" in *The Lord of the Rings*. In response, Tolkien writes "that by a strange chance" as he was beginning to read her letter,

---

42. Tolkien's attitude to laughter is not idiosyncratic but part of a fantasy tradition. See Martin, "God and Laughter," 4–12.

43. Rutledge, *Battle*, 133.

44. Bernthal's introduction, "Light from an Invisible Lamp," also foregrounds this letter. See Bernthal, *Sacramental*, 1–20. This letter has also been written about well by Spirito.

45. Tolkien, *Letters*, 578–80.

INTRODUCTION

another arrived from "a man who classified himself as an unbeliever, or at best a man of belatedly and dimly dawning religious feeling . . . but you, he said, 'create a world in which some sort of faith seems to be everywhere without a visible source, like light from an invisible lamp.'"

The second letter prompts Tolkien to recall meeting an art historian (whose name he had forgotten), who reminds Tolkien that his own art is built on the traditions of others. Tolkien likens this reply to Gandalf's reminders of the presence of the past, but then he also writes this reply to Batten-Phelps and the agnostic correspondent:

> Of his own sanity no man can securely judge. If sanctity inhabits his work or as a pervading light illumines it then it does not come from him but through him. And neither of you would perceive it in these terms unless it was with you also. Otherwise you would see and feel nothing, or (if some other spirit was present) you would be filled with contempt, nausea or hatred.

Tolkien gives no further explanation of this profound insight, except to quote Gollum's reaction to *lembas*; "dust and ashes" surely reminds any Catholic of both Lent and why unworthy reception of the eucharist is, to use understatement, "unhealthy." Wood is not wrong to see *lembas* as "clearly reminiscent of the eucharist wafer,"[46] nor is Bernthal wrong to connect this "waybread" to "wayfarers,"[47] a traditional name for Christians sojourning through our world. Yet of course *lembas* cannot signify the full range of meaning conveyed by the "blessed sacrament." Tolkien does not spell this out, but concludes the letter by accepting that *The Lord of the Rings* "does not belong to me," and by praising Batten-Phelps as one of the novel's "best friends." It is in her footsteps that the following reading attempts to walk. We cannot leave the path or story that Tolkien sets before us for an allegorical destination of our own preference, however noble or sublime. Nor can we ignore the many moments on the journey in which the hobbits' road meets the wider world of truth that surely exists.

Tolkien's Catholicism and worship of the one Triune God was both an essential guide and enduring consolation for him on this journey, and lesser spiritual wayfarers like ourselves must notice the truths Tolkien recovered. These are not abstract, however, and God Himself is ultimately our Friend, Brother, and Father, a King before Whom we happily bend our knees. Tolkien himself learned from Gerard Manley Hopkins that "the only

46. Wood, *Gospel*, 3.
47. Bernthal, *Sacramental*, 259.

just literary critic is Jesus Christ, who admires more than does any man the gifts He Himself has bestowed."[48] To justly appreciate Middle-earth, and our world, we have no choice but to recover His way of truth and life. As all hobbits must learn to sing in order to find their way, the one road goes ever on, but we start learning its true beauty, and destination, by beginning to walk. There is no finer companion for this walk than Samwise Gamgee.

---

48. Tolkien, *Letters*, 183. See Hopkins, *Correspondence*, 8.

Book One

1. A LONG-EXPECTED PARTY: "EVERYONE'S INVITED"

To introduce the Spirit needed to sustain this walk, a Spirit that Sam embodies, *The Lord of the Rings* opens with "A Long Expected Party." For some, this chapter is easily dismissed as "trivial" or "childish," at best a bridge to the novel's prequel, *The Hobbit*; even, perhaps, "somewhat tiresome."[1] One might also be disappointed that Sam makes only a brief appearance. Early in the chapter, Sam is given a longer introduction than most of the novel's major characters, but in an intentionally humble way, through the voice of his father, Hamfast (from Old English meaning "stay at home"), widely known as "the Gaffer." Whereas Frodo (Old English for "wise"[2]) became an orphan young after his parents were "drownded" (as Hamfast tells us), for Sam the voice and words of his father recur often, usually resulting in recovery of humility.

Sam's words in my chapter title here are indirectly quoted, as Hamfast tells us of Bilbo's forthcoming birthday party: "Our Sam says that everyone's going to be invited to the party." These words happily evoke the spirit of the present occasion but also suggest more universal application. Unexpected profundity in simple Sam's plain words will be something we come to expect. Everyone has a birthday, and the significance of these days is more than personal. Hamfast, likely often home teaching Sam the skills needed to be a gardener, also tells us that Sam has long been "crazy about stories of the old days." The "Gaffer" would caution:

---

1. Rutledge, *Battle*, 53.
2. Hammond and Scull, *Lord of the Rings*, 624.

> *"Elves and Dragons,"* I says to him. *"Cabbages and potatoes are better for me and you. Don't go getting mixed up in the business of your betters, or you'll land in trouble too big for you,"* I says to him.[3]

In an important sense, Sam learns his lesson well, never forgetting the authority of his "betters" nor the importance of potatoes, or "taters," which he will cook during a crucial part of the hobbits' journey. Yet it is his affection for both Frodo and the Elves, and fearlessness of dragons (and worse), that will make Sam so important to the "business" of the novel.

The Hobbit began with "An Unexpected Feast," so there is both a clear connection and obvious difference to the earlier text. We wonder: who has long expected this novel's party? Is it Bilbo, the beloved hobbit hero of our youth, now about to celebrate his 111th birthday? Or is it Gandalf, the wandering magician who has again arrived in the Shire, again bringing fireworks sure to entertain? Yet even if we have not read our way to the fourth section of this new novel's prologue, which tells the true story of how Gollum first got the ring and the true nature of his "riddle contest" (which had developed a fair bit in Tolkien's own mind since the initial publication of the novel), this first chapter gradually makes us aware that this new novel, though the same "age" as *The Hobbit*, is a much changed world.

The key marker of this change is the "magic ring" that we recall Bilbo winning from the strange creature Gollum in their game of riddles. We smile at Bilbo still having fun with it, appearing before the Shire to give a birthday speech, then slipping on the ring and suddenly disappearing, just as he did before with Gollum. Yet a note of pride does sound in the strange, ambiguous praise that Bilbo gives the shire-folk in his speech—"I don't know half of you half as well as I should like, and I like less than half of you half as well as you deserve"—but our concerns rise when Gandalf confronts Bilbo and suggests strongly that the hobbit no longer needs this "magic ring." "It is mine, I tell you. My own," Bilbo responds, before revealing the depth of his desire: "My Precious. Yes, my Precious." Gandalf says exactly what every reader of *The Hobbit* must think: "It has been called that before . . . but not by you." He does not say who said it, but Bilbo of course knows: "Even if Gollum said the same, once." Even as we are suddenly jolted into awareness of the likeness of the two former opponents of the riddle game, Bilbo's own violent potential is shocking as he again rebukes

---

3. As here, each quotation from *The Lord of the Rings* is from the chapter in the novel being considered.

Book One

Gandalf, his longtime friend and guardian: "'I won't give my Precious away,' I tell you. His hand strayed to the hilt of his small sword."

Happily, Gandalf does persuade Bilbo to give up the ring, though at this point in the story we cannot understand how significant this is, nor why it is that, as Bilbo agrees, "a spasm of anger passed swiftly over the hobbit's face." If we have read the novel's original preface, we have also heard Tolkien recount the true story, which was not revealed in *The Hobbit*, of how Gollum, originally a hobbit named Sméagol, first acquired the ring. Tragically, he murdered his friend, Deagol, to get the ring after it was found in the river where the two were fishing. Gollum's stated motivation, "It's my birthday, and I wants it," is surely meant to sound silly and childish, but it might also be seen as the primary motive of so much adult war: greed, and the certainty that one's own existence, and one's desire, is more important than the life of another, even of a supposed friend.

Three birthdays are compared and contrasted at the start of *The Lord of the Rings*: Bilbo is turning 111, and we begin to suspect numerology related to looking out for number one, but his nephew Frodo, who will be one of the main characters in this new novel, is turning 33. In Hobbiton this is known as "coming into the age of maturity," and readers cannot help but think of Christ's ministry. But there is also an obvious difference here: Christ dies at 33, whereas Bilbo's quest is just beginning. Gollum's birthday story is clearly much darker but also poses a key religious question: did Christ die hoping to save even wicked sinners who have committed humanly irreparable crimes? This is not a children's question, of course, but it may be part of why Gandalf is so interested in Bilbo's "true" story of what happened so long ago in the cave where he first met Gollum. Bilbo eventually gives up the ring and begins new adventures, singing:

> The Road goes ever on and on
> Down from the door where it began.
> Now far ahead the Road has gone,
> And I must follow, if I can,
> Pursuing it with eager feet,
> Until it joins some larger way
> Where many paths and errands meet.
> And whither then? I cannot say.

This song of the Road goes ever on, into both the past and future, but chapter 1 of this novel concludes with Gandalf giving the ring to Frodo but warning him not to use it. We wonder why, and gain a brief glimpse inside

Gandalf's mind when, as Frodo wonders whether he will ever see Bilbo again, the wizard replies, "So do I . . . and I wonder many other things." Readers are reminded of the great questions of life raised at every birthday: Why am I here? What is my life for? Implicit in such questions is religious wonder: Is there a God who has put me in this time and place for a purpose? Could God have "long expected" the birthdays remembered at the start of this novel? Here finally are both children's and adult's questions, but we are like Sam in being in a very dependent, unknowledgeable position if we were to attempt answers to these challenging questions. We wonder whether any authority in the world can give an answer, or protect us from the evil power now apparent in the ring. As the youngest hobbit, Pippen, will put it later in the novel, "Just who is Gandalf anyway?"

2. THE SHADOW OF THE PAST: "WHO INVENTED THE STORIES ANYWAY?"

The complexity of such questions,[4] and the painful presence of the past, becomes clear—both to Frodo and readers ready to sound the depths of this deeply serious novel—in its second chapter, "The Shadow of the Past." This chapter's title and ominous tone, especially in Jackson's film, cause many to fear the shadow as a symbol of evil, as in the mysterious shadow that passes along Bilbo's face when he finally gives up the ring. We are likely to be as dismayed as Frodo by how the past seems now to force him into an awful destiny: sacrifice his own life to destroy the ring or allow Sauron to regain it and destroy all goodness in the world. St. Augustine's famous conception of evil as the absence of Being is frequently cited, but perhaps Augustine himself might remind us that "shadow" should also remind us of the goodness and warming presence of God's Son, of light rather than utter darkness. In nature, shadow is an hourly changing reality, not to be feared but rather enjoyed as a place of rest. No one knows this more clearly than gardeners, and in this chapter, before any of the dark motifs, we first meet Sam, the hobbit who seems just an insignificant gardener, but who by novel's end becomes a powerful example of God's capacity to bring good out of evil.

This capacity is a key characteristic of the Creator imaged at the start of Tolkien's *Silmarillion*. At the beginning of this chapter, there is a seemingly unimportant scene where we first meet young Sam Gamgee, announced

---

4. The complexity of evil in Tolkien is written about well in Kreeft, "Wartime Wisdom."

simply as Frodo's gardener, having a pint at the Green Dragon Inn with Ted Sandyman, who at least has some pedigree as the Miller's Son (though academic readers familiar with Chaucer probably hear a joke on this). They are discussing the many strange rumors swirling about the shire, which Ted mocks, "I can hear fire-side-tales and children's stories at home, if I want to." Sam replies: "No doubt you can . . . and I daresay there's more truth in some of them than you reckon. Who invented the stories, anyway? Take dragons now."

Ted is not to be persuaded, but with this unassuming question, Sam Gamgee begins the key role he will play through the novel: friend to Elves and all things faërie, the voice of hope who allows us to remain enchanted even in the midst of darkness and the serious evil of dragons. Bernthal explains this key role well, seeing that "in Sam we see how the heart forms the imagination allowing him to see things that others miss."[5] Sam has long prepared for this role and knows, for example, of the "Gray Havens," a place we will actually see at the end of the novel. From there the Elves are returning to their homeland in the West: "Sailing, sailing, sailing over the Sea," sings Sam, "half chanting" while "shaking his head sadly and solemnly." This simple gardener seems like Tolkien himself, the master of *mythopoesis* for whom the stories of *The Silmarillion* were "the work of his heart,"[6] for "of all the legends that he had heard in his early years such fragments of tales and half-remembered stories about the Elves as the hobbits knew, had always moved him most deeply." As Tolkien's narrator then adds, "Sam had more on his mind than gardening." But perhaps it is first the humble, existential reality of gardening that allows Sam's mind the freedom to dream of Elves.

Gandalf is himself an important historical character in the "legends" loved first by Sam. Known first by the name Olórin and in service to the good "Ainur" who are also the servants of God, in this novel Gandalf is presented first as a guide who has been away for a few years, completed difficult research, and now will conduct one final test to confirm his hypothesis. When he dramatically throws the ring in the fire, it is light and heat that reveal hidden words etched into the Ring, in the language of Mordor; Gandalf translates them as, "One ring to rule them all / and in the darkness bind them." Thus it is revealed that this is the one ring of power by which

---

5. Bernthal, *Sacramental*, 168.

6. As Tom Shippey titles his chapter on *The Silmarillion* in Shippey, *J. R. R. Tolkien*, 226–63.

Recovering Consolation

Sauron will try to rule all. There is an obvious parallel to the Anglo-Saxon chiefs who crafted rings to verify fealty in the battlefields very real in their time, but the reality most modern Christians hear is the parallel to Satan, who seeks to eternally enslave humanity in the darkness of hell. As is usual with Tolkien, the allegory is not exact, but certainly there seems clear applicability. As noted in the preface, Melkor's similarity to Satan seems the most obvious biblical connection in Tolkien's mythology, and both the specific and general applicability of the novel's conception of evil seems confirmed when Gandalf tells Frodo: "Always after a defeat and a respite, the Shadow takes another shape and grows again."

Yet even as the approaching darkness appears so ominous due to the finding of the One Ring and the return of Sauron, enchanted readers also see glimmers of light. Even the frightening verses on the "one ring" are part of "a verse long known in elf-lore" that contradicts or at least qualifies the absolute fear meant to be inspired by the "one ring." The full Elven verse reports of a number of other rings, sadly telling of nine that ensnared men "proud and great," but there is clearly more than one ring, and Sauron's power is not absolute. Most significantly, there are three Elven rings, "fairest of all," that Sauron has "never touched" nor "sullied." Gandalf warns that even these could be threatened if Sauron triumphs, but clearly this possibility could yet be prevented. Thus Sauron cannot be the absolute lord of all the rings, which begs the central question raised by the title of the novel: who *is* the Lord of the Rings?

This key section thus raises the central theological question that we would expect from Tolkien's letters on the novel being, at heart, about God. Appropriately, it leads to the passage which seems most directly to speak of God's continuing presence and influence within Middle-earth. Gandalf emphasizes the objectively evil nature of the ring, which itself seeks to return to the master that made it, and so it is accurate to say, in describing how the ring left Gollum in the cave with Bilbo, that "The Ring left him." Yet,

> behind that there was something else at work, beyond any design of the Ringmaker. I can put it no plainer than by saying that Bilbo was *meant* to find the Ring. And *not* by its maker. In which case you were also *meant* to have it. Which may be a comforting thought.

It *is* a comforting thought, despite Frodo's initial, fearful response, if one adopts the logical, philological thought typical of both Gandalf and his maker, Tolkien; for something to be *meant*, there must be a Meaner; for this to be beyond the maker of the ring itself, this must be someone who logically can only be God. Gandalf "can put it no plainer than that" because that is the limit of Tolkien's theological mythopoesis, though he does explicitly tell Frodo, "You have been chosen." Biblically literate readers, such as Fleming Rutledge, easily recall how "all through the scriptures we see lowly, insignificant, and untried persons who are commandeered into the Lord's service through no wish of their own."[7]

God's continuing presence as Ilúvatar, the illuminator, is also suggested in a number of other ways. Whereas Peter Jackson waited until the prologue to his third film before revealing it, Gandalf here retells the sad story of Gollum first murdering for the ring. As Sméagol the hobbit he murdered his friend Deagol, who had fished up the ring, because, Sméagol rationalized—with the selfish, childish mind that has caused so many wars—"Because it's my birthday, and I wants it." Yet Gandalf thinks "there is some chance" of Gollum's "cure before he dies," and this hope comes from the unchanging reality of light within him. Despite the aversion of Gollum's own eyes and will to the light of sun, moon, or stars, Gandalf marvels:

> Even Gollum was not wholly ruined. He had proved tougher than even one of the Wise would have guessed—as a hobbit might. There was a little corner of his mind that was still his own, and light came through it, as through a chink in the dark: light out of the past. It was actually pleasant, I think, to hear a kindly voice again, bringing up memories of wind, and trees, and sun on the grass, and such forgotten things.

Even the dim light of interior memory preserves the possibility for Gollum of what Tolkien calls "recovery" in "On Fairy-Stories": "It was in fairy-stories," Tolkien there reveals, "that I first divined the potency of the words, and the wonder of the things, such as stone, and wood, and iron; tree and grass; house and fire; bread and wine."[8]

This insight leads Gandalf to what, by novel's end, emerges as one of its driving narrative motifs. Speaking of Gollum, Gandalf further tells Frodo: "My heart tells me that he has some part to play yet, for good or ill, before the end; and when that time comes, the pity of Bilbo may rule the fate of many." Pity, the virtue so important in medieval fairy stories such

---

7. Rutledge, *Battle*, 67.
8. Tolkien, "On Fairy-Stories," 60.

as *Gawain and the Green Knight*,⁹ and so derided by modern Nietzschean supermen, has always been close to Gandalf's heart. As a "maiar" in service to the "Ainur," the mythological beings who co-create Middle-earth with Ilúvatar, *The Silmarillion* tells us that "Olórin" learned from them "pity and patience," so that "in later days he was the friend of all the children of Ilúvatar, and took pity on their sorrows; and those who listened to him awoke from despair and put away the imaginations of darkness."[10] Pity has always been also the heart of Gandalf's interest in hobbits, and we will hear several times in the novel when Gandalf stresses the long-term consequence of the pity that Bilbo showed to Gollum.

Again we note the similarity to Tolkien's own thought, for he tells us in his letters that the "third age" of his mythology is "hobbito-centric" because it is "primarily a study of the ennoblement (or sanctification) of humility."[11] No one in the novel exemplifies this more than Sam Gamgee, and hence it is no surprise that this crucial second chapter, with revelations so fearful to Frodo, closes with the comical scene of Gandalf discovering Sam "eavesdropping" on his conversation with Frodo. Again there is evasive wordplay, as Sam pleads, "There are no eaves in Bag-End," yet to mistake him as a simple gardener is, typologically, to repeat the error that Mary Magdalene makes after Christ's resurrection. Tolkien is too precise an artist for it to be a coincidence that Sam's first word to Gandalf and Frodo is "Lor," "Lor" being a colloquial diminutive for "Lord" common in British English. Sam, in what again can be no coincidence, repeats the colloquialism to again remind us of his and Tolkien's mutual love for the Elvish tales that dominate the first two ages of Tolkien's mythology: "Lor bless me, sir, but I do love tales of that sort."

"Sam-wise" is Old English for "half-wise,"[12] and *The Lord of the Rings* will develop in many ways the wisdom of Sam's heart versus the simplicity of his head. Sam is close to the heart of both Gandalf and Tolkien, even though his head cannot understand much of what he has heard. He

---

9. Clearly, a key text for Tolkien. The main achievement of Tolkien's first academic appointment was a scholarly edition of *Gawain* with E. V. Gordon. After finishing *The Lord of the Rings*, Tolkien devoted one of his few public academic lectures, the W. P. Ker lecture of 1953, to *Gawain*. Tolkien also made his own translation of *Gawain* into Modern English, which was published posthumously. Both Tolkien's translation of *Gawain* and Ker Lecture on *Gawain* were reprinted as edited by Christopher Tolkien in 2021.

10. Tolkien, *Silmarillion*, 18.

11. Tolkien, *Letters*, 343.

12. Hammond and Scull, *Lord of the Rings*, 39.

is simply thrilled to accompany Frodo on what readers now know will be a most dangerous quest. We might call this "courage" but Sam's heart expresses more the enthusiasm of enchantment. As Sam exclaims in the chapter's last line, "Me go and see Elves and all! Hooray!" Tolkien's narrator informs us that just after shouting this Sam "burst into tears," but again the meaning here is clarified by the novel's end, when Gandalf will remind us that "not all tears are evil."

3. THREE IS COMPANY: "ELVES, SIR!"

Sam does not have to wait long to fulfill his enchanted desires. After the sublime, serious motifs raised in chapter 2, "Three's Company" seems to be the first of the novel's "travel chapters," where the hobbits move along the path of their quest. Yet this chapter's tone is leisurely, comic; Gandalf's power seems much more limited, for example, when he advises Frodo, "And see that Sam Gamgee does not talk. If he does, I really shall turn him into a toad." Much simpler questions thus begin the chapter: where and when should Frodo go? When he should go redeems the birthday motif darkened by Gollum's tragic origins; in an act of childish sentimentality, despite the time-sensitive dangers now revealed, Frodo enjoys one final summer in the shire, before leaving on what he calls "our birthday." Following Bilbo has clearly become important to him, but wary readers might also wonder if he is following Gollum. Frodo is unsure, though, of where to go, until finally his decision seems related to his humble gardener, Sam. He sets out for Rivendell, where

> "I will take Sam to see the Elves; he will be delighted." He spoke lightly; but his heart was moved suddenly with a desire to see the home of Elrond Half-Elven, and breathe the air of that deep valley where many of the Fair Folk still dwelt in peace.

However insignificant the average, suspense-driven reader finds this chapter, especially compared to the previous one, there is no better illustration of the fundamental difference between Tolkien's faërie-fiction and Jackson's film. Viewers of that film cannot forget the fearsome sniffing of the Black Rider searching for the hobbits, or the terror that grips Frodo as he reaches for the ring in order to become invisible; this moment does occur in Tolkien's novel, though in the novel Frodo does not slip on the ring. Instead, Frodo again turns to Sam, who recalls a recent conversation in which his father, the "Old Gaffer," had described just the sort of black rider whom they have just seen. Sam seems to calm Frodo, who advises himself to be "more careful on the road." The hobbits are learning the deeper significance of Bilbo's walking song, which they had sung earlier in the chapter and happily remembered Bilbo's sense of adventure, of where the "one road" out of the Shire could lead; now, they also are learning of the danger down many roads.

But the memory here does more than console; it also leads to Frodo's own first poem of recovery. In stanzas considerably more complex than Bilbo's simple walking song, Frodo sings that, on their road, the hobbits may meet "tree and flower and leaf and grass . . . apple, thorn, and nut and sloe . . . mist and twilight, cloud and shade." It is these fundamental realities of life, as Tolkien promised in "On Fairy-Stories," that will be experienced anew, rightly, on this new fairy adventure story. Recovery of such will itself be a consolation that sustains these hobbits for their entire journey.

When the hobbits actually meet the Elves, the consolation of Elvish song becomes even more magical. The hobbits can't understand the Elves' language, yet "the sound blending with the melody seemed to shape itself in their thought into words they only partly understood." Here is the first stanza as Frodo heard it:

> Snow-white! Snow-white! O Lady clear!
> O Queen beyond the Western Seas!
> O Light to us that wander here
> Amid the world of woven stars.

The lasting effect upon the hobbits goes way beyond any aesthetic of hedonism or even wonder. In times of great danger or fear, the hobbits will repeat the invocation that the Elves repeat throughout the song: "O Elbereth! Githoniel!" Understanding to whom these words refer, the "Ainur" who fashions the Elves out of the stars, seems almost secondary to the words' sound and beauty. With the Elves, poetic song seems almost light itself, enchanting the hobbits even as it allows them to know, by experience, the light of God.

Thus, it seems almost anticlimactic when Gildor, the Elves' leader, approaches and laughs at the strange sight of the hobbits abroad. When told of the Black Riders, Gildor offers them "company," an obvious expansion of the chapters' title, an offer that consoles each of the hobbits but especially Sam, who "walked along at Frodo's side, as if in a dream, with an expression on his face half of fear and half of astonished joy." Here is the already noted dual nature of Sam, enchanted in his heart even as his head fears the unknown. Things truly become wondrous, though, when the Elves are gathered in the wood and together "burst into song." For then, "suddenly under the trees a fire sprang up with a red light." Readers familiar with the opening of *The Silmarillion*, the "Ainulindalë," will recognize this as the "secret fire" of Ilúvatar, but the young hobbits are simply awestruck.

Afterwards, Sam remembers it as "one of the chief events of his life," but he can describe it only by analogy to gardening: "Well, sir, if I could grow apples like that, I would call myself a gardener. But it was the singing that went to my heart, if you know what I mean." Further echoing Tolkien's own view of Sam, as noted in the preface, here the Elves "smile at him and said laughing, 'Here is a jewel among the hobbits.'" Perhaps here theological typology is justified:

> It is notable that Sam chooses *apples* for particular mention. This may be a hint that the Elves are carrying around with them the recollection of the Garden of Eden in its pristine state, embodying the hope and longing of the world for its redemption from the serpent. The Elves singing surely suggests a connection to the transcendent world. Perhaps it is not too much of a stretch to recall that, in the gospel of John, the risen Christ comes to Mary Magdalene in the form of a gardener.[13]

Simple Sam is unlikely to take such a comparison seriously, but anyone remotely aware of transcendent meaning in Tolkien can hear this as the climactic moment of this chapter, one that literally and figuratively gives the hobbits light for the journey ahead. Tolkien further gives us a fairly long conversation between Frodo and Gildor, but its wisdom is minimal compared to the songs already sung. Frodo knows the proverb, "Do not go to the Elves for counsel, for they will say both no and yes," and indeed Gildor can say little other than what already seems obvious: Frodo should not "go alone," and should expect to find "courage" for the journey in unexpected places. Both bits of advice have already been taught in the chapter, but as readers we learn to expect multiple meanings of even clichéd motifs and chapter titles such as "Three's Company." As a scholar, Tolkien was surely aware of the commonplace *forma tractatus* technique of medieval art, wherein an artist would repeatedly fashion structures of three to indicate traces of the Trinity in the world created by the one living God.[14] This

---

13. Rutledge, *Battle*, 69.
14. As explained in the preface above, through reference to Allen, *Ethical Poetic*.

chapter is far too merry to abstractly present such concepts, but its songs do offer divine light, and chase away the fearful shadows of the past by recovering present joy and promising future peace.

4. "A SHORT-CUT TO MUSHROOMS": "I MUST SEE IT THROUGH"

With so much attention on Sam and the Elves in chapter 3, it is unsurprising that chapter 4 focuses instead on the other two hobbits who will be companions to Frodo for most of the book (though not as constantly as Sam). Pippen is first noted as the selfish young hobbit who would have eaten all the bread left behind by the Elves, leaving none for Frodo, if Sam does not save him some. Yet it is also Pippen who serves as diplomat, speaking for the other hobbits, to introduce them to the chapter's primary example of goodness, Farmer Maggot. It was this hobbit farmer from whom Frodo had stolen mushrooms years ago, and his dogs who had been pledged to kill Frodo if he ever set foot again on this land. There is another fearsome presence throughout the chapter, though, as the Black Rider heard and described in the previous chapter actually appears here, on the road that the hobbits have left to avoid him. It becomes very unclear how the hobbits will be able to make it to the ferry to Buckland, where Frodo had said he was going after leaving Hobbiton, but Farmer Maggot offers to conceal them in the back of his wagon and drive them there himself.

What appears to be the Black Rider approaches, but in an early, minor example of "eucatastrophe" or the sudden turn to joy, this rider turns out to be their old friend Merry, playing a practical joke which causes everyone to laugh. In one last happy turn, before leaving to ride home, Farmer Maggot gives Frodo one final gift, packed carefully by his wife: a freshly cooked basket of mushrooms, whose aroma is the final sense that the chapter appeals to. After so much fear of the sniffing Black Rider, the air is again not only safe but also sweet to smell. Despite knowing what the ring has done to the human beings who have degenerated into the Black Riders, finally the chapter reaffirms that Nature, and human nature, is good; as Genesis 1 states repeatedly, it is "very good."

Yet it is not humans, but the hobbit Sam, and the Elves, whose nature is the focus of the beginning of this chapter. Very early we hear Frodo tell Sam the real danger of their quest: "Most likely neither of us will come back." Sam then reaffirms the commitment made in chapter 2 to Gandalf when we first met him, but now described mainly as a memory of his conversation with the Elves:

> *Don't you leave him!* they said to me. *Leave him!* I said. *I never mean to. I am going with him, if he climbs to the Moon; and if any of those Black Riders try to stop him, they'll have Sam Gamgee to reckon with,* I said. They laughed.

So while the Elves have physically departed, their presence is more than just felt; their essence is heard, and we can say with Sam: "Wonderful folk, Elves, sir! Wonderful!"

Yet the Sam who speaks these words is not the same simple gardener that we had known before he actually met the Elves. Frodo perceives this, looking at Sam, as he is "half expecting to see some outward sign of the odd change that seemed to have come over him." To Frodo, Sam's face seems "unusually thoughtful," and what is "more on his mind than gardening," becomes even more interesting when Sam tries to put it into his own words:

> I don't know how to say it, but after last night I feel different. I seem to see ahead, in a kind of way. I know we are going to take a very long road, into darkness; but I know I can't turn back. It isn't to see Elves now, nor dragons, nor mountains, that I want—I don't rightly know what I want: but I have something to do before the end, and it lies ahead, not in the Shire. I must see it through, sir, if you understand me.

It would certainly be incorrect to say that Sam is no longer interested in Elves, but he does tell us that "they are quite different from what I expected—so old and young, and so gay and sad, as it were." Perhaps it is better to say, rather, that the Elves have permanently transformed Sam. From this point on, he has the tremendous courage possible only to those who retain interior awareness, even wonder, at the glory of God's light, but he also has a sad awareness of how proclamation of such light in the world of darkness inevitably involves sadness and pain. Sam remains enchanted, and this makes him more determined than ever, but he is also realistic about the cost, long before he understands what he himself must do to help Frodo's quest be successful.

Later in this fourth chapter we also see a flaw in Sam that often recurs, as he is irrationally mistrustful of Farmer Maggot because of the prior conflict with his master, Frodo. Simplistic errors of judgement do cloud Sam's head, perhaps as a result of his fierce determination to be faithful to Frodo.

RECOVERING CONSOLATION

Sam is a gardener familiar with physical nature and enamored of Elvish nature, but not intellectually aware of the complexity of either hobbit or human personality. This was an important part of his author's conception of his character; in one letter, Tolkien admits that at times, for some readers, Sam "irritates and even infuriates."[15] Nevertheless, he will faithfully serve Frodo, he will "see it through," and he remains the best guide we have to the enchanted quest upon which we have embarked.

5. A CONSPIRACY UNMASKED: "WE ARE YOUR FRIENDS"

With all three of the hobbits who will accompany Frodo on the dangerous quest now individually introduced, their collective identity as the first and fundamental "fellowship of the ring" can now be understood. Tolkien reveals this key role in a manner at once entertaining and enchanting, another early example in the novel of "eucatastrophe," or the sudden turn to joy. In this chapter we see that, far from this "turn" being a strictly literary or aesthetic "device," it actually is part of a recovery of the most fundamental human needs. So universal is this need, and so deeply felt amidst the widespread alienation of the modern world, which Eliot rightly termed a "wasteland," that many readers will remember the consolation of this recovery as the novel's primary theme: friendship.

Some sense of the importance of this theme is perhaps a prerequisite to enjoying the high comedy that ensues when the four hobbits arrive at "Crickhollow," the alleged "new home" in Bucklebury where Frodo has supposedly moved. Merry has prepared the home, and when natural potential conflict arrives because all are tired and dirty from the journey, Merry happily announces that there are three baths available. Pippen, unsurprisingly, lingers long in his tub, but also gives us a song of recovery to help us remember and appreciate this simple, everyday pleasure:

> Sing hey! for the bath at close of day
> that washes the weary mud away!
> A loon is he that will not sing
> O! Water Hot is a noble thing!

This song, "one of Bilbo's favorite bath-songs," continues in this same vein for three more stanzas, but its tenor is immediately clear. It is human

15. Tolkien, *Letters*, 464.

wisdom, vs. lunacy, to celebrate the simple consolations of life, and this begins with recovering an ability to exclaim with joy and gratitude for a simple gift such as "water hot." We chuckle at the mess Pippen makes during his song, splashing up so much water that he must mop up before eating, but the child within us sings along with him.

The greater gift of friendship is even more dramatically conveyed. Gathered after eating, this initial fellowship, led by Merry, gradually reveals that they have long known about Frodo's plan to leave the shire, and have even learned more than a little bit about the nature of the ring. Frodo seems shocked, and when Merry offers to introduce him to "our chief investigator," Frodo "expected a masked and sinister figure to come out of a cupboard." Instead Merry brings forward Sam, who "stood up with a face scarlet to the ears," making his master Frodo feel "quite unable to decide whether he felt angry, amused, relieved, or merely foolish." These conflicting feelings are not assuaged when Sam first responds by quoting Gandalf to justify his extensive espionage, which long preceded the day he was caught. Don't "go alone," Sam recalls the wise wizard saying, "No! Take someone you can trust."

Very understandably, Frodo tensely replies, "But it does not seem that I can trust anyone." Simple Sam just "looked at him unhappily," but Merry then gives one of the most eloquent statements of one of the novel's deepest themes:

> It all depends on what you want.... You can trust us to stick to you through thick and thin—to the bitter end. And you can trust us to keep any secret of yours—closer than you keep it yourself. But you cannot trust us to let you face trouble alone, and go off without a word. We are your friends, Frodo.

There is an obvious scriptural allusion or even application here—when Jesus insists that His disciples are not merely servants but also friends (John 15:15)—but even such sublime contexts cannot distract us from the beauty of friendship offered Frodo. Sam is the "chief" instigator of this gift, another sign of him being the "chief hero," but heroism in this novel is normally a collaborative effort. Merry's spoken words are Sam's Word, which he will prove for the rest of the novel.

6. THE OLD FOREST: "THERE'S MORE BEHIND THIS THAN SUN AND WARM AIR"

After such memorable examples of the goodness of nature (the mushrooms) and of hobbit nature (the initial fellowship), this chapter points further back to ancient nature, which Judeo-Christian theology traditionally terms "fallen"; it then concludes, though, with a key example, of the still greater and even more ancient mystery, also scripturally revealed, of original blessing. "The Old Forest" is a place, initially, that seems even more fearsome to many of the hobbits than the Black Riders. Merry's friend Fatty Bolgar, for example, prefers to stay in the house he has prepared for Frodo rather than venture into the forest; only at novel's end do we learn the consequences of this decision. Tolkien's deep love of trees was evident in his *Tree and Leaf*, but this chapter shows such ideas fully translated as literary enchantment. Here Tolkien recovers a *mythopoesis* designed both to shake any simple conception of dominion over nature, as many have misread *Genesis*, and also to console through the true goodness of ancient stewardship.

The forest does prove dangerous, but not in a "spooky" or "superstitious" way; rather, it seems a vivid example of the destructive consequences of violence against nature. Merry tells us that "the old bogey-stories" about the forest that "Fatty's nurses used to tell him" weren't true; he begins the chapter with a long narrative on the "bonfire glade," a burnt-out section of grass on the edge of the forest where hobbits past had burnt trees. Use of nature in this way has been basic to civilization throughout history, but this now common cultural theme is here given, by Merry, a *mythopoetic* twist. The hobbit "bonfire," in which they burned thousands of trees, came after the trees had risen up and "attacked the hedge." What exactly this means is unclear, but in the story we do hear the Tolkien who thought *Macbeth* insufficiently poetic because Birnam Wood did not itself, without the aid of hidden soldiers, rise up against the tyrant.[16] Here, Merry explains,

> The Forest is queer. Everything in it is so much more alive, more aware of what is going on, so to speak, than things are in the Shire. And the trees do not like strangers. They watch you. . . . I have only once or twice been in here after dark, and then only near the hedge. I thought all the trees were whispering to each other, passing news and plots along to each other in an unintelligible language; and the branches swayed and groped without any wind.

---

16. See how Tolkien contrasts fantasy and drama in Tolkien, "On Fairy-Stories," 50–52. On *Macbeth*, see Shippey, *J. R. R. Tolkien*, 192.

BOOK ONE

They do say the trees actually move, and can surround strangers and hem them in.

In addition to the trees, there are other "queer" things in the forest, and something has made paths that eventually lead the hobbits in the direction they do not want to go: towards the "Withywindle" river, "the queerest part of the whole wood—the center from which all the queerness comes, as it were."

The painful presence of the trees is felt most by Pippen, the youngest and most childish of the hobbits, who covers his ears before exclaiming, to the trees, "Oi! Oi! I am not going to do anything. Just let me pass through, will you!" Frodo tries again to inspire the hobbits with another walking song, but it fails, ending abruptly on the words "must fail" for here "the air seemed heavy and the making of words wearisome." Nevertheless, the hobbits go on, and we go happily with them, aware that beyond the wonder of art exists the wonder of nature itself. In this "old forest," ancient stories and mysteries become again present, embodied in figures never to be forgotten.

For the hobbits themselves, the scariest of such figures is surely "Old Man Willow," whom they meet near the "Withywindle," a river lined with willow trees, after they lie down sleepy in the hot day sun. Suddenly Merry and Pippen are trapped inside a tree, leaving Frodo helpless until Sam has the bright idea of setting the surrounding grass on fire. "Put it out! Put it out!" twice begs Merry, for the Willow itself, Merry further cries, "will squeeze me in two if you don't. He says so!" Sam starts to stomp out the fire, but Frodo begins to run about frantically, hollering, "Help! Help! Help!" Suddenly a new song is heard, coming from "back in the Forest."

Someone "was singing a song . . . carelessly and happily, but it was singing nonsense." At least, that is how it first sounded to the hobbits, but then the voice rose up loud and clear and burst into this song:

> Hey! Come merry dol! derry dol! My darling!
> Light goes the weather-wind and the feathered starling
> Down along under Hill, shining in the sunlight,
> Waiting on the doorstep for the cold starlight,
> There my pretty lady is. River-woman's daughter,
> Slender as the willow-wand, clearer than the water.
> Old Tom Bombadil water-lilies bringing
> Comes hopping home again. Can you hear him singing?

Those familiar with the music of Ilúvatar at the start of *The Silmarillion* may see the multiple forms of light present in this song, and literary critics might note that the full song is fourteen lines, the length of a sonnet, the most traditional poetic form, but it is arguable that the appropriate critical response is very simple, and given directly by the text: "Frodo and Sam stood as if enchanted."

Who is this guy? That simple question has become one of the central cruxes in Tolkien Studies, but all the many extra-textual theories seem unverifiable. Intratextually, we hear the wonder of music and see the gift of light. Tom is a merry looking fellow, with "a blue coat" and "brown beard" and face "red as a ripe apple," if a bit awkward, "stomping along with great yellow boots on his thick legs, and charging through grass and rushes like a cow going down to drink." But none of this odd appearance seems to matter as he frees the hobbits from Old Man Willow, for whom, Tom says, I "know the tune." Tom then invites the hobbits to his home, and goes ahead to prepare. When the hobbits arrive, they and the novel's readers hear and sing together, in a communion that becomes explicitly plural, perhaps the novel's clearest and thus most consoling song of recovery:

> Now, let the song begin! Let us sing together
> Of sun, stars, moon and mist, rain and cloudy weather,
> Light on the budding leaf, dew on the feather,
> Wind on the open hill, bells on the heather,
> Reeds by the shady pool, lilies on the water:
> Old Tom Bombadil and the River-Daughter!

Wonder thus both diminishes and awakens questions, but even Tolkien's narrator gives only a one sentence comment on this extraordinary song. Hearing it, "a golden light was all about" the hobbits.

7. IN THE HOUSE OF TOM BOMBADIL: "MOONLIGHT AND STARLIGHT AND THE WIND OFF THE HILLTOP"

The well-lit nature of Tom's house is stressed several more times as the novel continues. The room where the hobbits enter, initially, is "filled with the light of lamps swinging from the beams of the roof; and on the table of dark polished wood stood many candles, tall and yellow, burning brightly." Before we come to the mysterious identity of Tom himself, there is the perhaps even more puzzling identity of his wife Goldberry, the "river-daughter." Again wonder silences inquiry; when she looks at each hobbit and smiles, Frodo exclaims, "Fair lady Goldberry"; the narrator further explains that Frodo is feeling his heart moved with a joy that he did not understand. He stood as he had at times stood enchanted by fair Elven-voices; but the spell that was now laid upon him was different: less keen and lofty was the delight, but deeper and nearer to mortal heart; marvelous and yet not strange.

Frodo is soon singing a song of recovery, after first suggesting again the "sudden turn to joy" that is the heart of eucatastrophe: "Now the joy that was hidden in the songs is made plain to me."

After this primary consolation, again the hobbits turn to asking Goldberry, "Who is Tom Bombadil?" Presumably she knows, but her answer is enigmatic: "He is." Because this is an important theological name of God in both the Old and New Testament, it is unsurprising that some readers interpret this answer as pointing to divine allegory. But Goldberry also insists that Tom does not own his land, and Tom himself tells us he is not master of the weather, which together seems to rule out any possibility that he is a divine incarnation. On the other extreme of interpretation, it is true that Tolkien published poetry of Tom Bombadil long before writing *The Lord of the Rings*, and that several of Tolkien's children have confirmed that "Tom Bombadil" was the name of a doll in their home.[17] If Tom is neither powerful enough to be divine nor so passive as to be a children's toy, others have seen him as some sort of unfallen creature, full of "divine creative joy" like a Catholic saint such as St. Francis of Assisi.[18]

If we focus on what Tom does rather than who he is, he does not seem to have the morality of a saint but rather an almost selfish devotion to Goldberry. Yet Catholics familiar with Christ's frequent admonition to "be not afraid" hear the same as Goldberry and Tom often welcome the hobbits in a similar way. When Frodo, Pippen, and Merry go to sleep, all have nightmares; each regains peace, though, because of the protection afforded by Tom's house. Merry goes back to sleep aware that nothing can come inside Tom's house but "moonlight and starlight and the wind off the hilltop"—in other words, the peaceful recovery of the most basic elements of nature made by the Creator. Nothing seems more natural or good, though, than the peaceful sleep enjoyed by Sam; recovering another simple cliché, Tolkien's narrator tells us that "Sam slept through the night in deep content, if logs are contented."

---

17. Hammond and Scull, *Lord of the Rings*, 124.
18. Bernthal, *Sacramental*, 138.

Recovering Consolation

Perhaps the best answer on Tom's identity comes from Tom himself, after Frodo directly asks him the following morning. "Don't you know my name yet," Tom explains, then says more directly, "That's the only answer." Perhaps, as a number of critics have argued, Tom Bombadil is an absolutely unique, mysterious character who exists and has meaning solely within Middle-earth. Yet in no way does this diminish Tom's importance. In the same conversation with Frodo, Tom tells him that

> I am old. Eldest, that's what I am. Mark my words, my friends: Tom was here before the river and the trees; Tom remembers the first raindrop and the first acorn.... He knew the dark under the stars when it was fearless—before the Dark Lord came from Outside.

If Tolkien were an allegorical writer, and Morgoth is Satan, then Tom and Goldberry could be Adam and Eve before the fall; but there is not enough detail to sustain the allegory, so Tom exists as a completely unique figure known only through Tolkien's mythology.

Rather than any aesthetic or theological explanation, the chapter closes with a dramatic scene that especially impresses Frodo. Tom tosses the ring in the air, slips it on his finger and then the hobbits are shocked: "There was no sign of Tom disappearing!" Frodo is almost indignant, for Tom has made "so light of what even Gandalf thought so perilously important." Yet then Frodo totally forgets Gandalf's advice, and puts on the ring to make sure it still works. When Merry cannot see him, Frodo is delighted, but somehow Tom can still see him and tells him to take off the ring, for "your hand's more fair without it." Again, there is the suggestion of the holy goodness of all that God has made. Finally, Tom teaches the hobbits another song of recovery which they can sing out in their hour of deepest need:

> Ho! Tom Bombadil, Tom Bombadillo!
> By water, wood and hill, by the reed and willow,
> By fire, sun and moon, harken now and hear us!
> Come, Tom Bombadil, for our need is near us!

Calling in need to Tom Bombadil could easily be likened to calling on the name of Jesus, as Christians have traditionally done in times of danger. Another explanation of Tom's identity is given by Sam, though, at the end of the next chapter: Sam laments having "to take leave of Master Bombadil" for "he's a caution and no mistake. I reckon we may go a good deal further and see naught better, nor queerer." Whether because of the source, casual use of the "being" verb or odd diction, this explanation is very rarely noted even by those directly investigating Bombadil's identity. Yet there are clues to Sam's profound understanding both in the novel and in the historical philology that Tolkien knew so well.

Sam will open Book VI with the sentence, "We're in a fix master, and no mistake." We can save this sentence's complex philology until then, but "no mistake" both there and here, with reference to Bombadil, likely connotes an intentional, providential act of God. This is part of the very broad reflection on divine sovereignty at the heart of Tolkien's *legendarium* but here, with Bombadil, this theology can be clarified through Sam's seemingly odd use of "caution." Sam probably means not just a "warning"—for Tom has been more life-preserver than lighthouse for the hobbits—but rather the Middle English word "caucioun" which meant "guarantee" or "pledge."[19] Often used in conjunction with "bail" or the freeing from imprisonment like Tom's rescue of the hobbits from Old Man Willow or the Barrow-wight, in a broader medieval sense Bombadil could be taken as a pledge of the Creator's goodness, a sure guarantee of the superiority of good over evil. This sense fits with the rest of Sam's explanation of Bombadil; in the rest of our long journey, we will meet no good "better," nor no single example of the unique or "queer" nature of each of God's creatures.

8. FOG ON THE BARROW-DOWNS: "WHERE ARE MY CLOTHES?"

As the hobbits leave the House of Tom Bombadil, all seems peaceful. In Frodo's dream the night before leaving, "a far green country opened before him under a swift sunrise"; outside, even when the hobbits awake, "everything was green and pale gold." The consolation recovered through Tom will have lasting consequences for the hobbits, but as they travel on, beyond the old forest, they will also face many elements of fallen nature that remain dangerous. The most fundamental of these, and the most applicable to our world, is death. "Ainulindalë" speaks of "the gift of death," the purpose of which has been darkened by Melkor, but Tolkien is also in the Christian tradition in which "death is the last enemy to be defeated" (1 Cor 15:26). The two conceptions of death, as gift and enemy, can of course be understood not as contradictions, but according to their roles in human life. Early, arbitrary death is evil, causing the absence of the fullness of life, but

---

19. See the entry for "Caucioun" in *Oxford English Dictionary*, 360.

no one should die afraid to be with God in eternity. Yet many do feel great fear of death, and this chapter faces that fear.

Before facing the natural reality of death itself, this chapter first recovers, in the mythopoetic sense central to Tolkien's work, the physical reality of elements in the natural world which remind us of death. "Fog" is of course natural in sea-side communities, whose inhabitants often have a love-hate relationship to fog; the reasons for hate are obvious, but one also can't discount, for example, a commonplace of Nova Scotia, where one often hears, "Fog is for lovers." In this chapter, though, we see an even more dangerous natural consequence of fog: losing touch with one's companions. Frodo is suddenly separated from his three friends; lost in the fog, he can no longer see them. This is especially upsetting because he is walking on "downs," large mounds of earth that, in Tolkien's Britain, are known to be ancient burial grounds. Naturally pleasant to climb on the outside, inside they include the grim reality of death. That reality, of course, is not simply historical or particular, but nearly universal, and certainly a natural reality that threatens these four young hobbits. Tolkien calls the grim specters that the hobbits meet in this place the "barrow-wights"; "wight" is the common Middle English word for "people," and hence a term that specifically applies to the ancient dead, but would also include those persons who fall into its broad category today.

The "fog on the barrow-downs" means that Frodo must face death alone, as all people must. Tolkien's portrayal of this fearsome topic is again both mythopoetic and a recovery of the most fundamental realities of nature. It is also highly dramatic; searching for his lost friends, Frodo cries out, "Where are you," but the reply, "Here . . . I am waiting for you," comes not from a hobbit but rather a creature who is almost as dangerous an enemy as the other hobbits are comforting friends. "Trembling" Frodo looks up, and sees

> a tall dark figure like a shadow against the stars. It leaned over him. He thought there were two eyes, very cold though lit with a pale light that seemed to come from some remote distance. Then a grip stronger and colder than iron seized him. The icy touch froze his bones, and he remembered no more.

Frodo has been captured by a "barrow-wight" who, though too gruesome to be described precisely, seems to be a long dead person still gathering wealth in a hole in the ground.

A ghastly opposite of hobbits, in other words, but perhaps the most terrifying moment of the whole ordeal comes as Frodo turns on his side and realizes that there beside him are Sam, Pippen, and Merry, faces looking "deathly pale," and "across their necks lay one long naked sword." Frodo can't know if they are dead or alive, but just as the hobbit walking songs give inspiration to go on, here "an incantation" is heard to make one think death the only reality:

> Cold be hand and heart and bone,
> and cold be sleep under stone:
> never more to wake on stony bed,
> never, till the Sun fails and the Moon is dead.

The nameless singer goes on for a few more lines but there is no need to quote and ponder the meaning; cold, dull despair makes Frodo feel as though he has been "turned into stone."

Yet even here the recovery of natural reality returns Frodo to an interior awareness of his soul's real nature. For "though his fear was so great that it seemed to be part of the very darkness around him," Frodo "found himself as he lay thinking about Bilbo Baggins and his stories." As Bilbo did at crucial moments in *The Hobbit*, Frodo finds "a seed of courage" inside himself and, feeling the ring in his pocket but resisting the temptation to put it on, "with what strength he had he hewed at the crawling arm near the wrist, and the hand broke off." Frodo then is able to sing the rhyme that Tom Bombadil had taught him, concluding, "Come, Tom Bombadil, for our need is near us!"

A "sudden deep silence" follows, and soon then is heard the consoling sound of Tom singing. Then the atmosphere of the barrow suddenly changes: "Light streamed in, real light, the plain light of day." This crucial recovery is soon followed by Tom banishing the "old Wight," then with Frodo carrying the other three hobbits outside to the top of the barrow-mound; there, with treasure taken from the barrow, Tom "laid them all on top in the sunshine" and then sang another song of recovery:

> Wake now my merry lads! Wake and hear me calling!
> Warm now be heart and limb! The cold stone is fallen;
> Dark door is standing wide; dead hand is broken.
> Night under night is flown, and the Gate is open!

As so often in the novel, the poetic song is crucial; from it comes eucatastrophe, as "to Frodo's great joy" the other hobbits revive. They are shocked by their own appearance and want their old clothes, but Tom hints towards an even fuller recovery: "You've found yourself again, out of the deep water." He tells them to "run naked" over the grass, and no biblical reader can help but think of Eden. As with Lewis's *Perelandra*,[20] perhaps this is another scene that Jackson or his actors did not want to film.

Those who cannot accept that fairy stories recover fundamental reality may not take seriously the sudden turn to joy caused by Tom Bombadil. Yet in my opinion, there is no greater mistake in Jackson's film than the decision to entirely omit Bombadil. One can defend the decision from the filmmaker's point of view, for Tom is unnecessary to the plot, but perhaps Jackson's deeper problem is how to explain that the ring is a trinket to Tom but very dangerous for everyone else in Middle-earth. Yet this omission is one of many ways in which Jackson's film becomes much darker than Tolkien's novel. Death is dark, fearsome, and cold—as I personally discovered in my own near-death experience—but brighter still is the reality of God's love. However partially we can understand this, Tom Bombadil embodies this love for the hobbits. We will not see Tom again in the novel, but how seriously we should take him is again strongly suggested at novel's end when Gandalf, after all the adventures and excitement of Frodo's ring, travels to speak with Tom for *two years* before himself leaving Middle-earth. That is a conversation we'd all love to hear, but we don't; perhaps it concerns divine light beyond even Tolkien's great imagination.

9. AT THE SIGN OF THE PRANCING PONY: "WE SURELY AREN'T GOING TO STAY HERE FOR THE NIGHT, ARE WE SIR?"

After all the scary, supernatural, but sublimely consoling events of the past three chapters, this seems at first to be a return to the safety of human civilization. After all, Tom Bombadil himself has recommended the inn where they will rest the night, the "Prancing Pony" at Bree, and Tolkien's narrator provides an extensive history early in the chapter to explain that Bree has long been a place where hobbits and men—whatever their distant ethnic origins—have lived together happily. Yet the chapter also seems the first clear sign that, as he himself has stressed, Tom Bombadil's power does not extend beyond his own land. In Bree, the dark danger facing the hobbits

---

20. This second novel in Lewis's "Cosmic Trilogy" takes place on a pre-fallen Venus; hence its characters are nude.

is glimpsed briefly, lurking in the shadows, but an exceptional human is also introduced who will become very important to the success of Frodo's mission.

This chapter's ability to both comfort and remind us of real danger is shown first through its names. Names are always polyvalent signs in Tolkien's art, as philological scholars continue to reveal, but one does not need advanced degrees in linguistics to begin catching some of the meaning here. The innkeeper Barliman Butterbur, a hobbit with a long lineage connected to material stuff that matters both to hobbits and men, is recommended by Bombadil and a friend of Gandalf. The innkeeper provides both the needed barley and comfort of butter needed for every hobbit breakfast and beer, and is a burr in the side of evil that he steadfastly refuses to serve. Frodo attempts disguise through the name "Mr. Underhill," intending suburban banality that has a long history amongst the families of Bree. However, readers cannot so soon forget the spooky wonders that lay under the hills of the novel's previous three chapters, and it is a sign of the novel's most extraordinary human's arrival that "Strider" instead calls Frodo by his true name, "Mr. Baggins." Sam, Pippen, and Merry are largely happy to again have the simple comfort of ale, yet a clear sign of our present distance from the enchanted world is the contrast between the "Green Dragon Inn," where we first heard Sam disputing Ted Sandyman's sense of fairy stories, and the "Prancing Pony" in which both hobbits and humans strut their animals for show, oblivious to the more substantive realities around them.

For much of the rest of Book I, we don't know much of what has gone on in Sam's mind since he slept "like a log" in the house of Tom Bombadil. We hear no fairy songs in the inn, but in stark contrast a slightly tipsy Frodo gives us a very clichéd, very modern pub drinking song, on the "man in the moon." The crowd cheers and sings along, but swiftly turns away from the hobbits, and treats them as strange outsiders, when Frodo suddenly disappears. This surely surprises readers as well, for Frodo was aware of no imminent danger and thus would not seem to be tempted to put on the ring himself. The more likely conclusion to draw seems to be that the ring moved itself onto Frodo's finger, perhaps reaching out to evil men within the inn to reveal its presence. Two shadowy men slip out the door right after this happen, and readers rightly and naturally suspect that they are in league with the Black Riders.

One cannot help but also be suspicious of the dark stranger who now comes forward to speak to Frodo. Sam especially will long be suspicious of

"Strider," but readers here must also tremble with wonder at how he knows Frodo's real last name, "Baggins." Does "Strider" say it with the sarcasm that reminds us of the Black Riders? Of course, we eventually learn that "Strider" is not this man's real name either, but one whose word can be trusted beyond that of any human the hobbits will meet.

Within the history of hobbits and men that opened the chapter, we heard about "Rangers," wanderers who are "taller and darker than the Men of Bree and were believed to have strange powers of sight and hearing"; they sound mythological. Yet, here at the end of this seemingly most unenchanted, prosaic rest at a clichéd country pub, in the midst of danger far darker than the cave where Bilbo first met Gollum, the hobbits have found this jewel among men, a Ranger who will prove to be one of their dearest friends.

10. STRIDER: "I NEVER HEARD NO GOOD OF SUCH FOLK"

Very few readers today would come to this chapter unaware of who "Strider" becomes. Surprise, though, is not Tolkien's purpose here. The "hidden hero" motif is almost the only way a truly heroic, ultimately noble royal hero could be introduced so early in the novel. "Aragorn," as we first learn to rightly name him in this chapter, must have spent many years hidden, growing in humility, in order to avoid the arrogance and corruption that afflicts most human political leaders; most humans in general, even a literary critic must humbly add. The main interest here, rather, is how the hobbits react to the hidden image that hides the real man who "Strider" actually is. We have come to expect Sam, the hobbit already most sanctified by humility and pity, to be our guide to enchantment, to see through false appearance and recover Elvish consolation. Yet this is not some magical power hidden in Sam; he needed Bombadil as much as any hobbit in facing hidden dangers, and in this chapter Tolkien goes out of his way to show that Sam can make a mistake, of the "head" rather than the "heart," in mistrusting "Strider" even when the hobbits are truly in need of this extraordinary human's help.

This point is particularly emphasized by being made twice at key points in the chapter. After Strider strongly suggests, while laughing about the "Baggins" and "Underhill" ruse, that he knows the "secret" the hobbits are bringing out of the Shire and the danger it poses, he offers himself as a "guide" and protector for the long journey ahead of them. An extraordinary offer, but Sam clearly rejects it:

> With your leave Mr. Frodo, I'd say *no*! This Strider here, he warns and he says take care; and I say *yes* to that, and let's begin with him. He comes out of the Wild, and I never heard no good of such folk. He knows something, that's plain, and more things than I like; but it's no reason why we should let him go leading us out into some dark place far from help, as he puts it.

Sam's words here perfectly capture his intellect's mixture of plain-speaking honesty—which may remind us of the Sermon on the Mount's admonition to avoid oaths and instead say only "yea, yea," or "nay, nay" (Matt 5:37)—with an agitated long-windedness likely caused by Sam's deep desire to protect Frodo. Even after a letter from Gandalf seems to confirm Strider's goodness, Sam remains skeptical:

> How do we know that you are the Strider that Gandalf speaks about? . . . You never mentioned Gandalf, till this letter came out. You might be a play-acting spy, for all I can see, trying to get us to go with you. You might have done in the real Strider and took his clothes. What have you to say to that?

One must remember that these impertinent questions are posed by a small, simple hobbit to a much larger, stronger, and taller man who has long made his living as a "Ranger" dealing with the most dangerous creatures of the wild. Though Sam's words here could charitably be described as a lesson in caution, they also teach us much about courage.

Even here, then, Sam consoles us, but surely the main source of enchantment in the chapter is the letter from Gandalf. It too is mainly prosaic, but it is signed with a mark we see for the first time—the simple Elvish rune, which "Appendix E" of the novel presents as a "cert" for the letter "G"—which, if one knows ancient Elvish runes, certifies Gandalf's identity as a good friend of the Elves. But by far the most important part of the letter is its middle verse, which comes after the cert is used for the third time in a post-script and the key naming of the hidden hero: "His true name is Aragorn." Sounding very much again like old Elvish lore, Gandalf continues:

> All that is gold does not glitter,
> Not all those who wander are lost;
> The old that is strong does not wither,
> Deep roots are not reached by the frost.

Recovering Consolation

> From the ashes a fire shall be woken,
> A light from the shadows shall spring;
> Renewed shall be blade that was broken,
> The crownless again shall be king.

Even experienced readers of Tolkien are likely to focus here on mainly the first two and the last two lines; they are aware that "Strider" is the hidden king referred to, and it is natural to read this portion as part of the puzzle which Gandalf's letter purports to solve: the real identity of Strider. In lines 3–6, though, there is the far deeper mystery of ancient enchantment and consolation. Taken on their own, without direct reference to Aragorn, the lines recover concrete awareness of ancient roots, ashes, light. The lines console by asserting that the past reality of such things cannot be erased, even though roots are often hidden from the physical eye, warming fires seem to go out, and darkness can seem to be all encompassing.

Against such apparent truths, there *is* here the reality that Strider *is* Aragorn, true man and true king. The letter leaves Sam "undaunted," as already noted, but very logically Aragorn argues, "If I had killed the real Strider, I could kill you." Furthermore, he adds, "If I was after the Ring, I could have it—NOW!" Like the other major authority figures in this novel, Aragorn here has a brief moment when he is tempted by the potential power of the ring, tempted to grab it and make himself a new "dark lord," however bright he might first appear. Aragorn passes this test, however, and instead offers the hobbits as profound a consolation as any passage in the novel: "I *am* the real Strider, fortunately . . . I am Aragorn son of Arathorn; and if by life or death I can save you, I will."

A "long silence" follows this key line, and Sam becomes especially quiet, speaking only one more simple sentence for the rest of the chapter. We can't know exactly what Sam is thinking, but recalling his earlier silence after Elvish lore we can guess that his spirit is again stirred. Aragorn's promise is Elvish, recovering the most consoling truths free to any man's, or hobbit's, inner life. There is an important Christian application here, for Aragorn is a true king who will serve the King of kings who taught us that "greater love hath no man" than to "lay down his life for his friends" (John 15:13). Ultimate truth of this kind, which the medievals call "anagogical," does not need to be spoken clearly yet. Here, faced with the dark danger of the Black Riders preparing to assault them in the night, it is more than enough that in his final two lines in the chapter, though he has returned to seeming a simple good friend who can laugh and joke with the hobbits, Aragorn speaks the word that must sustain them all on this journey: "hope." This cardinal theological virtue makes them "all fall silent," and all able to sleep—perhaps as soundly as Sam slept in the house of Tom Bombadil—safe now with a real man, a true friend who will rule and protect them with the wisdom and courage of a real king.

11. A KNIFE IN THE DARK: "I WOULD LIKE TO HEAR MORE ABOUT ELVES; THE DARK SEEMS TO PRESS ROUND SO CLOSE"

It is natural for many to take this as the climactic or most significant chapter of Book I. Here, the Black Riders finally catch up to Frodo, and give a wound which eventually results in him leaving Middle-earth. The wound would have been immediately fatal without Elvish medicine, and even Aragorn seems powerless to stop it. In Jackson's film, much of the scene has a nightmarish quality intended to haunt, and even when Frodo slips on the ring the Riders can see him and deliver the horrible blow; the knife finds its mark despite the dark. So dark is the chapter that Sam makes the request I have put in my chapter title here: "I would like to hear more about Elves; the dark seems to press round so close."

When "Strider" responds to Sam, the tale he tells is that of "Beren and Lúthien." Today, there are many clear, external signs of how important this tale was to Tolkien. His letters call this "the chief" of all the tales in the first age, and the "main link in his mythology,"[21] but why? First published posthumously, as chapter 18 of the 1977 *Silmarillion*, this love story is about the first marriage of a human male (Beren) and an elfin/maia (Lúthien) and produces descendants such as Eärendil, who uses the silmaril (a jewel containing the original light of Ilúvatar) to navigate a route home to Valinor, and Elrond, whose own daughter Arwen will marry Aragorn. Tolkien first worked on the tale during his World War I convalescence, and his son Christopher recalls listening to the tale as his first experience of his father's mythopoesis, particularly remembering a fearsome cat named Tevildo.[22]

Though this cat does not appear in later versions of the story, the aid of non-human characters is highlighted by the hound Huan, perhaps the most loyal and heroic beast in all of Tolkien's writings. In the earlier versions of the story, Lúthien is called "Tinúviel," or nightingale, the romantic

---

21. Tolkien, *Letters*, 209.
22. Christopher Tolkien, "Introduction," in Tolkien, *Beren and Lúthien*, 17.

Recovering Consolation

name also used by Aragorn to introduce the story in this chapter of *Lord of the Rings*. As Christopher Tolkien's 2017 edition of the text highlights, the elf dance in the forest so important to Beren and Lúthien seems taken from the biography of Tolkien's patient, determined courtship of his wife, Edith. Perhaps this is part of why, in the most obvious use of allegory in Tolkien's work, he wrote on their common gravestones (she had died two years before him) so that under his name was simply "Beren," while under his wife's was "Lúthien."

The full rationale for this extraordinary "gravestone allegory" is probably reserved for the eternal world[23] where, Tolkien's poem "Mythopoeia" tells us, poets "still will make, not being dead."[24] Yet why does it appear *here* in *The Lord of the Rings*, and in such length? Jackson uses the moment to introduce Arwen, the future, Elven bride of Aragorn, but the parallels to Frodo's trials are less apparent. An obvious application, though, and surely intended, is how Beren and Lúthien show great courage, face great danger, and do succeed in escaping the dungeons of Morgoth to give again divine light to their people. In this crucial sense, Aragorn's re-telling of the Beren and Lúthien tale does give much needed light to the hobbits. They have been brought to Weathertop, an ancient lookout, to physically see and avoid the Black Riders. Though that intent fails, once Frodo puts on the ring and the Riders can see him, the tale told by Aragorn allows the hobbits, and readers, to see this physical danger in the light of ancient history, and with hope for eternity. Divine light, recovered here, will console the hobbits at many other points in their journey.

In this light, the title of the chapter can be re-interpreted and re-evaluated. As with so many titles and names in Tolkien's always complex literary philology, multiple further meanings are suggested beyond the literal fact that a Black Rider's knife in the dark stabs Frodo, almost fatally. Aragorn's tale is a glowing knife in the dark much as Bilbo's sword, "Sting," glows when aware of nearby danger. Aragorn's sword, though physically broken, is soon to be reforged in fulfillment of ancient legend, and the courage he will show, ready to lay down his life for his friends, is to be a light for the hobbit's entire journey. Sam does not fully grasp this, just as Beren thought of regaining the Silmaril as a means to appeasing an angry father-in-law and winning his wife, rather than a light for his future offspring. The light of Beren and Lúthien, though, is treasured in Sam's heart, and its meaning

---

23. See Maillet, "Meeting Somewhere in Truth."
24. Tolkien, "Mythopoeia," 90.

shines upon Frodo, despite his physical wound, even in his eventual return to the eternal world.

12. FLIGHT TO THE FORD: "WHAT IS THE MATTER WITH MY MASTER?"

The light of Beren and Luthien to explain the chapter title "Knife in the Dark" is supported early in the next chapter, "Flight to the Ford." Aragorn describes how Frodo's knife slashed the black garment that now lies on the ground, but then comments, "More deadly to him was the name of Elbereth." The title of this chapter also has a simple literal reference, the concluding chase of Frodo by the Black Riders to the Ford of Bruin. But again, this action is only a small part of the chapter, and the really important part of the chase occurs *in* the Ford. There, Elvish art again plays a critical role in the action. Frodo would not have arrived at the Ford, furthermore, if not riding on an Elf-Horse given by Glorfindel. This elf, sent by Elrond from Rivendell, bears the name of a famous elf from the city of Gondolin, which so long remained secret to save itself from the forces of Morgoth. The present Glorfindel would not have been able to find and help the hobbits without a "chance" accident that reminds us of the finding of the ring. While out searching for "athelas," the ancient herb medicine of the Elves, Aragorn finds something "very strange," a "pale-green jewel" that he calls "a Beryl, an elf-stone." Readers do not know yet that Aragorn himself wears a similar stone, a reminder that, as he will tell us in this chapter, his "heart dwells in Rivendell," with Arwen.

Though Elvish art and legend are thus central in the chapter, for much of it Samwise is "choked with tears," stricken with grief over Frodo's wound. He cannot comprehend much of what happened on Weathertop, partially because he could not physically see it, and in this chapter he barely manages, "in a low voice," to ask, "What is the matter with my master?" Here it is Aragorn that must exhort Sam not to despair, but amidst all the bad news the old pony of Bill Ferney has "improved wonderfully" and shown "affection" for his "new masters, especially Sam." While Aragorn is away scouting, this pony leads the hobbits to new paths where they are given a concrete reminder of another old story, that of the three trolls who almost ate Bilbo and the dwarves in *The Hobbit* before the sun turned them to stone. Frodo soon laments them "forgetting their family history," but the story is given a mock serious introduction; the hobbits here first fear that they have found a cave hiding living trolls from the North, but Aragorn soon returns to amend Frodo's critique by adding that they have forgotten "all they ever knew about trolls." He points out that one of the stone trolls "has an old bird's nest behind his ear," and the subsequent laughter leads Sam to find his voice.

Sam delivers an eight-stanza story-song, with seven lines in each stanza, which pokes fun at another Troll frustrated at losing dinner. The presumed meal in Sam's song, however, seems to be Tom Bombadil! Tom gives this troll the slip, actually booting him in the butt, in the climactic sixth stanza:

> But just as he thought his dinner was caught,
> He found his hands had hold of naught.
> Before he could mind, Tom slipped behind
> And gave him the boot to larn him.
> Warn him! Darn him!
> A bump o' the boot on the seat, Tom thought
> Would be the way to larn him.

The partially nonsense rhymes in line five of each stanza and the colloquial diction clearly recall the songs of Bombadil, and Tolkien will republish this as "Troll Song" in his 1962 poetry collection, *Adventures of Tom Bombadil*,[25] but here the other hobbits are again amazed by Sam's creativity. "There's more stored in your head than you let on about," Merry says even before the troll song, and after it Pippen can only wonder, "Where did you come by that, Sam?" Sam's own answer is "inaudible," but Frodo comments that he is "learning a lot about Sam on this journey," and further wonders whether this "conspirator" may yet turn out to be "a wizard—or a warrior?" "I don't want to be neither," Sam protests, and again laughing readers must happily agree.

Sam's song of trolls, who had seemed so scary in *The Hobbit* until recovery of the sun suddenly consoled, turns Book I's conclusion from the tone of fearful worry over Frodo's wound back to enchanted wonder. Frodo's "flight to the Ford," on Glorfindel's white horse, recreates this wonder. The strength of this white horse foreshadows the "white rider" whom Gandalf will become on Shadowfax—the great white horse eventually on the elf-ship that leaves the Grey Havens at novel's end—and "anagogically" would be related to the "White Rider" of the book of Revelation. Within the novel, though, what happens in the Ford is very present, concrete, Elvish art:

25. Tolkien, *Adventures of Tom Bombadil*, 20–22.

At that moment there came a roaring and a rushing: a noise of loud waters rolling many stones. Dimly Frodo saw the river below him rise, and down along its course there came a plumed cavalry of waves. White flames seemed to Frodo to flicker on their crests, and he half fancied that he saw amid the water white riders upon white horses with frothing manes. The three Riders that were still in the midst of the Ford were overwhelmed: they disappeared, buried suddenly under angry foam. Those that were behind drew back in dismay.

This key example of eucatastrophe, we learn in the next chapter where Book II begins, was caused by the combined art of Rivendell and Gandalf. But beyond the Black Riders here Frodo sees "a shining figure of white light." If Catholics do no forget sacred history, which Tolkien here poetically prompts, we also see "the light of the world" who ultimately allows the merry songs of singers such as Sam.

Book Two

1. MANY MEETINGS: "GLORY AND TRUMPETS"

After so much adventure and danger in the last few chapters of Book I, Book II opens with a chapter of rest. This applies to readers and hobbits both, but most especially to Frodo as he recovers from the wound at Weathertop. Rivendell is the perfect place for doing this, "as Bilbo had long ago reported; 'a perfect house, whether you like food or sleep or storytelling or singing, or just sitting and thinking best, or a pleasant mixture of them all.'" Most of the "meetings" in our chapter title include Frodo, but the Elvish quality of Rivendell, home of the ancient Elrond, permeates the chapter. After Gandalf meets with the awakening Frodo and gives him a broader context for all that has happened so far, Frodo's next meeting is with Sam. Sam announces this theme with his characteristically concrete enthusiasm for all things Elvish:

> It's a big house this, and very peculiar, always a bit more to discover, and no knowing what you'll find around a corner. And Elves, sir! Elves here, and Elves there! Some like kings, terrible and splendid! and some merry as children. And the music and singing—not that I have had the time or the heart for much listening since I have been here. But I'm getting to know the heart of the place.

One does need a heart like Sam's to appreciate Rivendell, but even intellectually his words could be taken not only as a description of this "last homely house," but of all Elvish art, including *The Lord of the Rings* itself. As such, there is much to discover in this chapter of rest and reflection.

Gandalf often helps us understand the supernatural in the novel, and begins doing so here by confirming the reality of the dangers the hobbits have passed through. On the barrow-wight, for example, Gandalf tells Frodo: "That was touch and go: perhaps the most dangerous moment of all."

BOOK TWO

In case anyone confuses Gandalf with deity, however, Gandalf also explains to Frodo that he was late coming back to the Shire because he had been "captured"; no details are given here (they can be found in *The History of Middle-earth*, but Gandalf clearly states the main point: "There are many powers in the world, for good and for evil. Some are greater than I am.") We have already met some of these powers in the Barrow-wight and Bombadil, but Gandalf's focus here becomes Aragorn, whom both he and Frodo acknowledge as the "Ranger" who has saved the quest "from disaster." Sam still "has doubts" about "Strider," but this skepticism is not a mark against his Elvish faith, for few alive could grasp Aragorn's true greatness, simply because there are so few men like him; Gandalf tells Frodo, "There are few left in Middle-earth like Aragorn son of Arathorn. The race of Kings from over the Sea is nearly at an end. It may be that this War of the Ring will be their last adventure." The hesitant nature of Gandalf's words are not a sign of weakness, but of the humble honesty that he has long valued in hobbits like Sam. Even as Frodo recovers from his terrible wound, however, Gandalf does not shy away from clarifying the nature of the war they are now in. When Frodo asks whether Rivendell itself "is safe," Gandalf clarifies the stakes: "Yes, at present, until all else is conquered."

Here, actually in Elrond's home, much of Rivendell's goodness seems infinite and surely its spiritual if not physical aspects are unconquerable. The true good of friendship is again highlighted, as Gandalf also reports that Sam has been at Frodo's bedside throughout the recovery. After the introduction of several of the extraordinary features of this ancient Elvish home, Frodo gives another of the novel's great affirmations of friendship by fondly recalling Bilbo: "I would rather see him than all the towers and palaces of the world." In Rivendell, this wish is soon granted in the "Hall of Fire," perhaps the most purely Elvish space in this blessed place. Here there is always fire, but little other light. It is not heaven, for Bilbo himself cannot help but ask about the ring on seeing Frodo, and Gloin, one of the dwarves from the Hobbits, is also there reminding us that problems created by greed continue to exist in the world. But so much anxiety soon seems less real because of the reality of art. Before giving another long example of such in poetic legend, Tolkien vividly describes such art; alone again (Bilbo having returned to a corner to continue writing), Frodo feels "forlorn," but then hears the sound of the Hall of Fire:

> At first the beauty of the melodies and of the interwoven words
> in Elven-tongues, even though he understood them little, held

him in a spell, as soon as he began to attend to them. Almost it seemed that the words took shape, and visions of far lands and bright things that he had never yet imagined opened out before him; and the firelit hall became like a golden mist above seas of foam that sighed upon the margins of the world. Then the enchantment became more and more dreamlike, until he felt that an endless river of swelling gold and silver was flowing over him, too multitudinous for its pattern to be comprehended; it became part of the throbbing air about him, and it drenched and drowned him. Swiftly he sank under its shining weight into a deep realm of sleep.

Exceptional though this paragraph surely is, and as much as it could bear extensive commentary as a guide to Elvish art, in the novel itself it is easy to miss. In his dream, Frodo immediately hears, in the sound of Bilbo chanting, a long poetic account of the First Age's penultimate and perhaps greatest story of recovery and consolation: Eärendil the Mariner using the light of the Silmaril (inherited from Beren and Lúthien) to find sea-passage home to the Blessed Realm of Valinor. That place is as close to heaven, to full communion with God, as Tolkien's analogous art allows. The key place of Bilbo's poem in this chapter, superseding but also confirming the critical understanding of Elvish art in the preceding paragraph, allows us—if we attend to the verses—to recover ancient legend and experience directly the consolation of Elvish art. So significant within Tolkien's legendarium is this long poem that it must be read in full; but, we can glimpse a small bit of its light in a stanza that mentions Eärendil's wife Elwing (a direct descendent of Beren and Lúthien) and gives us the name of the jewel that contains divine light. The Silmaril is the main subject of the first age, as when Eärendil is lost at sea, and

> There flying Elwing came to him,
> And flame was in the darkness lit;
> more bright than light of diamond
> the fire upon her carcanet.
> The Silmaril she bound on him
> And crowned him with the living light,
> And doubtless then with burning brow
> he turned his prow;

Given such Elvish art, one wonders, especially given my thesis, where's Sam? The answer is at once simple—as Frodo leaves the Hall of Fire, Tolkien's narrator tells us that Sam stays behind, "fast asleep still with a smile on his face"—yet also profound, given how the chapter has developed the motif of dreaming as an artistic way of being more awake than "normal" consciousness allows. Introducing the Hall of Fire, Gandalf told Frodo, "Here you will hear many songs and tales—if you can keep awake." As Elrond introduces Bilbo, he implores him, "Awake, little master," to which the old hobbit is indignant: "Wake up! I was not asleep, Master Elrond. If you want to know, you have all come from your feast too soon and you have disturbed me—in the middle of making up a song." This is the song of Eärendil that Frodo hears in his dream, so it is safe to conclude that Sam also shares in the glory of Elvish art in the Hall of Fire. It is easy to forget him there, as it is to undervalue his role in the entire novel, but we can't forget the key role Sam has played in bringing Frodo to this point and aiding his recovery. When Frodo first woke up, Sam was thrilled that his hand was again warm and exclaimed, "Glory and trumpets!" Within the theology of Tolkien's mythology, where the music of the Ainur join with Ilúvatar to create all that truly is, Sam's words are a simple but true celebration of recovery, consolation, and enchanted joy.

2. THE COUNCIL OF ELROND: "A NICE PICKLE"

There are many other key moments in "Many Meetings," surely one of the greatest and most easily underrated chapters in the novel. Far beyond the literal meeting of Frodo and Bilbo to which the title seems to refer, readers meet so many ancient but still living figures in Tolkien's legendarium that are crucial to the Third Age, none more important than Eärendil. Comically, at one point, Pippen greets Frodo as "The Lord of the Ring"; Gandalf rebukes this childish silliness towards Sauron, but readers cannot help but notice that the novel's title must refer to another Lord who reigns over the plural (three!) rings that the Elves still employ.

Far more seriously, another crucial part of the motif of human and Elvish love is also developed in the chapter. As Frodo leaves the Hall of Fire, he hears an Elvish language song to Elbereth, the Ainur who with Ilúvatar made the Elves out of stars. Frodo then sees the "light of [Arwen's] eyes fall on [Aragorn]"; then Frodo "stood still enchanted, while the sweet syllables of the Elvish song fell like clear jewels of blended word and melody." Such moments may seem less important as we turn to a broad search for policy in "The Council of Elrond," the long second chapter of Book II which seeks to find how best to deal with the complex problems revealed in "The Shadow of the Past," the long chapter 2 in Book I of the novel.

RECOVERING CONSOLATION

These two key chapters are not "mere historical background" but rather "carefully narrated wisdom."[1] Most of this second long chapter functions as a "guide to Middle-earth" for anyone unfamiliar with the first and second ages of Tolkien's mythology. However, clearly emerging from the chapter is Elrond's proclamation that this is "the age of hobbits," the creatures whose existence was not known even to Tolkien himself when he wrote his early legends.

As Bilbo and Frodo enter the council, "behind them, uninvited and for the moment forgotten, trotted Sam." Until the very end of the chapter, we don't hear a word from him, though it is a clear sign of Tolkien's affection that Sam does get the last word in this meeting of powerful representatives of all the peoples of Middle-earth. Much of the early part of the chapter is told by Elrond, unsurprising since he lived it, though Frodo expresses the wonder that any must feel in the presence of Elvish longevity. Most notably, Elrond was there for "the last alliance of Elves and men," serving as herald for Isildur in the war at the end of the second age against Sauron. Elrond thus knows much about Sauron's aims for the ring of power, and of Isildur's failure to take the opportunity to throw the ring back into the fire of Mount Doom from which it was forged. However, there is also much that Elrond does not know about the rings' subsequent history; as the council proceeds, a number of speakers, representing "the free peoples of Middle-earth," supplement our knowledge of the history of Middle-earth.

We first hear from Gloin, a dwarf in *The Hobbit*, then from Boromir, a human who has come from the ancient kingdom of Gondor. Bilbo next recounts (for the first time publicly, it is noted) how he got the ring from Gollum, then Frodo tells of his own dramatic, more recent journey, pursued by the Black Riders. Finally, in the chapter's longest narrative, Gandalf explains that he was delayed from his planned travel with Frodo due to being imprisoned by Saruman, the once noble "head of his order" who now seems corrupt. Each of these narratives is fascinating and related in important ways both to the past that Elrond has lived and the future quest the hobbits are about to make.

Prominent Tolkien scholar Tom Shippey has written well on why such a long chapter of speeches, without much action, does not become dull.[2] Shippey notes both Tolkien's clear grasp of Middle-earth's history and the council speakers' diverse voices, but also how the chapter works to allow

1. Wood, *Gospel*, 79.
2. Shippey, *J. R. R. Tolkien*, 77–82.

Book Two

unlearned readers both a basic sense of relevant history and a living sense of the extraordinary fellowship about to be created. For at the end of the second age, the battle against Sauron was won by the "alliance of Elves and men," but here, now there will be a new fellowship of Elves, dwarves, men, wizards (actually maia spirits) and above all, though least in stature, hobbits. Each narrative in the chapter gives important insight into each kind of creature. Gloin the dwarf is almost exclusively concerned with his own people, of how a ring of power and deception by Sauron led them to awaken evil beneath Mount Moria; later in the chapter, Elrond will rebuke Gloin for not listening attentively to the other speakers. Pride is also the major problem of men such as Boromir, who (tragically, we later see) is not really persuaded here that the ring cannot be used as a weapon against Sauron. Yet prophetic lore about a returning king's "broken sword" and some unknown creature, the "Halfling," has made Boromir courageous enough to journey far north to the council. It is the innate, natural, god-given traits of each kind of creature that makes them important to this new fellowship. Thus it is the Creator's calling (or as Catholics typically call it, the "vocation") that Elrond speaks of when he welcomes them all; deciding what to do with the ring

> is the purpose for which you are called hither. Called, I say, though I have not called you to me, strangers from distant lands. You have come and are here met, in this very nick of time, by chance as it may seem. Yet it is not so. Believe rather that it is so ordered that we, who sit here, and none others, must now find counsel for the peril of the world.

Without resorting to public revelation, Tolkien could not present a clearer or more authoritative faith in the reality of Providence.

As the character longest and most clearly in the service of divinity, Gandalf has the longest narrative in the chapter. Much of it, as with Gloin and Boromir, concerns the main traits of the kind of creature he is; from the *Silmarillion* we know that Gandalf is a "maia," a spirit in service to the "Valar" (or "powers") whom the "Ainur," original co-creators with God, became once Middle-earth was physical, and not simply real in the mind of God. We know also that Sauron is, similarly, a "maiar" in service to a Valar, but in his case to the rebel Ainur first named Melkor then Morgoth.

But what of the creatures in Middle-earth also similar in nature to Gandalf, but on the same side of the ancient spiritual war? Answers to this question largely emerge through contrast to Saruman, often referred to as being once "the head" of Gandalf's "order." Yet Saruman "the White" has become multi-colored, and he scorns the original white that, Tolkien's poem "Mythopoeia" makes clear, has nothing to do with ethnicity but rather is suggestive of divine purity and simplicity.[3] Saruman mocks both Gandalf "the Grey" and Radogast "the Brown" (the often foolish nature Wizard who sent Gandalf to Saruman's castle) before explaining that white "serves as a beginning" but "it can be overwritten," and the "white light can be broken." Gandalf understands clearly the obvious problem with this choice, for then "it is no longer white." The argument here is not over color, or style; the white light referred to is that of the Creator, Ilúvatar, and Saruman's choice entails reliance on his own power (which he hopes to combine with the power of Sauron's ring) rather than the power of God. This is an illusory aim, of course, as becomes clearer in the novel when Gandalf returns, from spiritual battle with the Balrog, another ancient servant of Melkor, as "the White." Gandalf is still the same wizard as before, but then ready to lead the war of the Third Age.

Both Elrond and Gandalf insist, to Boromir especially, that the powerful cannot themselves use the one ring of Sauron without becoming corrupt, but this commonplace is then given its positive example through focus on the nature of hobbits. Comically, after hearing all the narratives, Bilbo offers to take the ring, saying, he "started this affair" and must now finish it. Bilbo has for the first time publicly told the true story of how he got the ring from Gollum, and his offer here is honest. Yet it is also naïve, and does not appreciate the true history of the ring; as Gandalf tells him, "IF you had really started this affair, you might be expected to finish it." But by this point in the chapter even the average reader, unfamiliar with the First or Second Age, knows that a much more ancient story is being told. This age will be the "age of Hobbits," for the simple reason that has caused Bilbo to think he must again be the ringbearer; Elrond explains, "Such is oft the course of deeds that move the wheels of the world: small hands do them because they must, while the eyes of the great are elsewhere."

Reinforcing the providential purpose that the Creator has for hobbits, especially to destroy Sauron's ring, Tolkien does not have the Council appoint Frodo to this fearsome task, nor does the hobbit proudly or heroically accept it. Rather we are told that Frodo's words come "at last with an effort,"

---

3. In "Mythopoeia," Tolkien presents the white light of God as the source for true artistic "sub-creation," which moves "from a single White / to many hues, and endlessly combined in living shapes that move from mind to mind" (Tolkien, "Mythopoeia," 87).

and he himself "wondered to hear his own words, as if some other will was using his own voice." Readers, recalling the sudden poetry of Sam in earlier chapters, could imagine that the voice that speaks is Sam's, but the quest to destroy the ring will require a more radical, even more humble reliance on the leading of divine providence, of trusting in God's will even when uncertain even of how to take the first step. "I will take the Ring," Frodo says, "though I do not know the way."

This way will not be alone, though, as this long chapter 2 ends in almost the same manner as "The Shadow of the Past." Here Elrond again discovers Sam, formally noting his indiscretion even while comically describing his service to Frodo: "It is hardly possible to separate you from him, even when he is summoned to a secret council and you are not." Sam has the last word, though, summing up the entire trouble caused by the ring with a word or expression known to every simple resident of the Shire: "A nice pickle we have landed ourselves in, Mr. Frodo!"

3. THE RING GOES SOUTH: "IF YOU DON'T LET ME GO WITH YOU, SAM, I'LL FOLLOW ON MY OWN"

As in Book I, a second chapter central to the novel's plot and themes is followed by what many dismiss as a "travel chapter," as the new Fellowship leaves Rivendell and heads towards Mt. Doom in Mordor. As this direction demands, however, there is very little of the Elvish beauty which lightened the hobbits' first journey outside the shire. Every step of this new journey will be hard, painful, and as the Fellowship attempts to travel through mountain passes, even greater dangers emerge than the Black Riders: freezing cold, large snow drifts, and the natural tendency to fall into depression or even despair after days and nights far from whichever comforts have, in what now seems to be the distant past, have sustained each creature in the company. For the most part, Sam does not stand out in this chapter, and there suddenly seems little time or space for the poetic, Elvish art they had so grown to love in Rivendell. Early in the chapter we have one final taste of this, as Bilbo gives them a six-stanza song, whose repetitive line, "I sit by the fire and think," hardly seems conscious let alone empathetic to painful journey the young hobbits are about to undertake.

The will of the entire Fellowship is both formed and challenged by this chapter's journey, but other themes also emerge that are part of the novel's central themes. As, for example, with the other chapter titles, here the precise diction and grammar suggest a broader idea than the obvious travel; the ring is the subject of its own sentence, which reminds us again of the ring's objective desire, beyond rational understanding, to return to its master. This chapter also reminds us that there are many elements of creation, sometimes long hidden, which had fallen in past rebellion against God. As Gimli the dwarf (son of Gloin) reminds us, speaking of the mountain which the company now tries to climb, "Caradhras was called the Cruel... long years ago, when rumor of Sauron had not been heard in these lands." Not even the combined wisdom and strength of Gandalf and Aragorn can safely navigate this path, and eventually the Fellowship must descend the mountain and turn to a "dark and secret way" that the two experienced leaders have not wanted to try first.

There are enchanted moments in the chapter, such as when Legolas the Elf scouts ahead by zooming across snow with his nearly bare feet barely touching the ground. But mostly concrete reality challenges the wisdom of any proverb; before he leaves Rivendell, Gimli answers Elrond's caution that one should not vow "to walk in the dark" before seeing nightfall by declaring his own bravery and the power of suffering to sharpen iron: "sworn word may strengthen quaking heart." "That's true too," as Lear puts it, but this journey is so harsh that one barely retains breath to speak. One of Sam's few comments, as they build a "shelter" to survive the snowstorm in the night, comically contrasts where they have travelled to in leaving behind the "last homely house" of Rivendell: "'Shelter!' muttered Sam. If this is shelter, then one wall and no roof make a house." Snow can be welcomed by playful children, but Tolkien is realistic enough to have Sam say, "Snow's all right on a fine morning, but I like to be in bed while it's falling." Sam's intellect, while far from brilliant, often shows a strain of common-sense realism or even satire, such as when he comments, on the delay in their journey south, "We'll just wait long enough for winter to come." In the snow, "it passed the skill of Elf or even dwarf," we learn, "to strike a flame that would hold amid the swirling wind or catch in the wet fuel." Gandalf's staff starts fires, and his "miruvor" or Elvish "cordial" warms their bellies, but he cannot stop the snow. Neither he nor Aragorn, any more than Tom Bombadil in his lands, is "weather-master."

There is one enchanting element of recovery that does console during the chapter. Bill, as Sam ironically calls the pony who is a much more faithful son than sadistic spy-master Bill Ferney of Bree, had "a great wonder of change" during his rest at Rivendell, where his coat became "glossy" and regained "the vigor of youth." Sam then argued that this poor pony should bear supplies on the journey, not because of renewed strength but because "that animal can talk." Tolkien's share in this apparent reminder of Narnia, and of his complex friendship with C. S. Lewis, seems affirmed when the narrator then comments: "So Bill was going as the beast of burden, yet he was the only member of the Company that did not seem depressed." We don't hear Bill talk during this harsh journey, nor even Sam talk to him; the closest we come to this, ironically, is when the pony makes a sad face when being asked to bear even more wood up the cold mountain. Yet Bill's silent service remains faithful despite hardship, and perhaps this is the chapter's true consolation. Sam does indirectly report one thing that Bill "says," and it is a memorable thought which also applies directly to the horse's new master: "If you don't let me go with you, Sam, I'll follow on my own."

This is true though the chapter ends with a harsh sentence: "Caradhras had defeated them." This "end," part of the many false conclusions that began with silly Bilbo proclaiming, "This is the end," simply remind us that the Company's journey is not simply physical, harsh and real though that is, but also spiritual. The spirit of Bill the Pony, and his new master Sam, strives on amidst the snow, simple and sure despite the uncertainty even of Aragorn and Gandalf. At the start of the chapter Sam responded to old Bilbo's hope for the traditionally consoling ending, "They lived happily ever after," with a realistic question of recovery: "And where will they live? That's what I often wonder." This wonder foreshadows the words Sam will speak to close the novel, but here they remind us of the spirit needed to reach that point. Here, now, Sam, Bill, and the rest of the Company will follow Gandalf to an even darker place, for their inner light is alive and, as we've already learned, where there's life there's hope.

4. A JOURNEY IN THE DARK: "MY HEART'S RIGHT DOWN IN MY TOES"

The deepening darkness of the journey becomes literal when the "darker path" known to Gandalf is revealed as a trip through the almost completely dark realm of Moria, an ancient dwarf kingdom *inside* one of the mountains in which they are travelling. The company is practically forced to enter this mountain when attacked by a slew of water snakes in a swamp near the mountain where they are wading, but the decision that Moria is the only way left open to travel towards Mordor had already been made by the

Company's leadership. While acknowledging that few would take this hard path by choice, the crucial question is asked before the snake attack, when Gandalf says: "Who will follow me, if I lead you there?"

Gimli, enthusiastic to see a famous dwarf kingdom, is the first to say yes. Aragorn quickly follows, but shows prophetic foresight in personally warning Gandalf against this path. The other man, Boromir, by contrast says, "I will not go," then calls for a vote of the whole company. Legolas does not want this path—unsurprising for an elf—but Frodo calls for delay of vote until next day, when better weather may mean that Gandalf then "will get votes easier." So Frodo clearly hopes Gandalf's choice will be respected, though the sudden appearance of first wargs then the snake renders any voting process moot. The point is not the value of authoritarian leadership, but the distinction crucial to authentic conceptions of both monarchal and papal authority: the authority of leadership based upon both wisdom and courage.

We don't hear how Sam would vote, and it seems apt when the chapter goes on to show him travelling through Moria, not at the end of the line—Aragorn assumes the "last shall be first" position appropriate to his unique role in the book—but rather in the middle, without any apparent agency. That is perhaps because he has the most agonizing and difficult choice of anyone at the start of the chapter. Gandalf points out the obvious, that Bill the pony cannot traverse the treacherous path inside the mountain, and at first insists that he will not desert Bill, after all the devoted service Bill has given. Gandalf is not unfeeling, and actually goes to Bill and speaks to the pony directly: "Go with words of guard and guiding on you. . . . You are a wise beast, and have learned much in Rivendell. Make your ways to places where you can find grass, and so come in time to Elrond's house, or wherever you wish to go." The extraordinary care of these words, and respect for the pony's free desire, helps us to understand the special bond later formed between Gandalf and his own horse, Shadowfax. Even this is not enough here to appease Sam, who argues that "it'd be nothing short of murder" to say goodbye to Bill here, with so much apparent danger around him. Gandalf is right to disagree, saying that Bill has as good a chance at safety as the company does, and indeed we do see the pony later in the novel! So Sam here again is clearly wrong, but it is ironic that he will also overestimate Gandalf's power over evil creatures. Yet Sam does not follow out of fear, but rather duty; as the Company clamors into the mountain, it is the inevitable conflict between passionate duty and freedom of choice (a major theme in the novel) that makes Sam tearily explain: "I had to come, Mr. Frodo. I had to come with you."

Sam's attitude to Bill, far from being "sentimental attachment" (though Boromir seems to have no use for it), is accepted through imitation by the novel's highest authority figure, Gandalf. Simple Sam thus exemplifies one of the novel's clearest echoes of the gospel, as Aragorn—servant-king to the King of kings—exhorts the Company to follow Gandalf in the famous, challenging, yet paradoxically comforting words of Christ: "Do not be afraid!!" Beyond courage, Sam further helps us to apply something that this chapter reminds us is also of the heart: friendship.

Christ tells His apostles, we cannot too frequently note, "I call you not servants" but "friends" (John 15:15); this verse is not directly quoted, but the point is made in this chapter in a way related to "moon runes," an ancient form of the philology that Tolkien practiced in his professional life. In Gandalf's second major physical illustration of Elvish art, after he first tossed the ring in the fire, here Gandalf shows how the Moon's light reveals the hidden cave door that will allow the Company to enter Moria. In this light, we see "the Tree of the High Elves," and other Elvish and Dwarvish emblems; there is also an inscription which reads, in part, "*pedo mellon a minno.*" Gandalf first translates this as "speak, friend, and enter"; Gimil thinks this "plain enough": "If you are a friend, speak the password, and you will enter." Gandalf then racks his brain, in vain trying to remember the password; finally, "laughing," he exclaims: "I have it! . . . Of course, of course! Absurdly simple, like most riddles, when you see the answer."

The answer is to simply speak the Elvish word for friend, "mellon." That is the password, and the *intellectual* error of Gandalf was one of mechanical translation familiar to all modern readers of ancient texts: the insertion of commas where none are intended. Emotionally, though, the riddle's simple truth has already been exemplified by the most humble of hobbits, Sam, in his affection for both Bill and Frodo. Gandalf does not note this, but just after solving the riddle he adds something that must puzzle most readers: "Merry, of all people, was on the right track." Yet one searches in vain to find Merry suggesting the right answer; what Merry did do, while Gandalf and Gimli were first considering the inscription, was ask a question: "What does it mean by *speak, friend, and enter*?" On the page of our text, Merry seems simply to be repeating what Gandalf and Gimli have already said, but the humble question of wonder should remind us of the spirit of Sam, whom we happily recall Merry introducing as "the chief conspirator" in the hobbits' fellowship of friendship.

Indirect example and influence are what we should expect from humble, simple Sam, though his voice is again directly heard after the further "leading turn" taken by Gimli. Inspired by Moria, chanting "in a deep voice," it is Gimli who suddenly gives the Company a new song for their long walk in Moria, a forty-six-line homage to Dwarvish legend and hard work. "I like it," immediately answers Sam, though it is the sound rather than the meaning of the words he has enjoyed; he adds, repeating a key line, "I should like to learn it. In Moria, in Khazad-dûm." The meaning he and the other hobbits will associate with the latter word becomes particularly tragic in the next chapter, but here it is the merry heart of Sam, united in friendship to Gimli, Gandalf, and the rest of the Company, that keeps them moving through this dark journey.

Late in the chapter Frodo will wish he had "never heard of Moria, or mithril, or the Ring," and even magical runes at the end of the chapter return Gimli's face inside his hood after they reveal that Balin is dead. All seems very dark, though Frodo is haunted by an echo of footsteps behind him, and by "two points of light, luminous eyes." Readers are probably right to interpret these signs as Gollum following the ring—though we can't know how he got into Moria—and it is true that eventually this most derelict hobbit will become a guide on the even darker path to Mordor. The spirit of Sam is absolutely necessary to Frodo's safety on that journey, and to the success of the quest to destroy the ring.

5. THE BRIDGE OF KHAZAD-DÛM: "WEEPING"

This is one of the shortest and darkest chapters in the entire novel. Correspondingly, as we would expect from all that we have learned so far, this is also the chapter in which we hear the least from Sam. No attentive reader can be surprised by Gandalf's famous demise here, which so clearly was foreshadowed when Aragorn forewarned Gandalf against entering Moria, and which sardonic readers might have predicted in response to Sam's assurance, also just outside Moria, that Gandalf would never fall to so base an evil creature as a warg. Yet nothing is more particular to a first-time reader of the novel, unaware of the eventual return of Gandalf the White, than the utter despair that must be felt when Gandalf falls into the abyss, apparently to be seen for the last time, toppled after being leg-whipped by the fiery

Book Two

Balrog, an evil creature so fearsome that even the orcs are frightened by its presence. For the first-time reader, perhaps the most memorable sound of this awful chapter is not the repetitive "doom, doom" of the drums announcing this horrible day of fate, but the sound of Sam "weeping" as the surviving company runs out of the dark cave and into the suddenly bleak air of light and freedom outside. This, of course, is the real emotion of the characters inside the novel, who so far as they presently know, have lost Gandalf forever. The wail of Sam weeping becomes the background song to the pounding drums—doom, doom—that sounds throughout this painful chapter.

Although the chapter does not give evidence of the Elvish inner life that has made Sam such an enchanting and often surprising character so far, there is a least one moment when he shows surprising physical valor and courage like that of Bilbo and Frodo. Early in the chapter, the Company interprets too late the dwarves' ancient texts to avoid repeating Dwarvish history by being trapped by orcs in the chamber of records, "Mazarbul." Sam is wounded on his forehead, but "a fire was smoldering in his brown eyes that would have made Ted Sandyman step backwards." Sam then acts on this hidden hobbitish courage when a fearsome orc-captain rushes toward Frodo, perhaps drawn by the ring, and spears him with such force that Frodo is pinned against a wall. We can later confirm that the *mithril* coat prevents serious injury, but Sam "with a cry" gives valiant defense; he "hacked at the spear-shaft, and it broke." We learn later that the mithril coat has prevented serious injury, but we should not underestimate the importance of Sam's action; if the spear had not been broken, only God knows what further damage it might have done. Within the novel, this action foreshadows the later moments when Sam's physical actions protect Frodo, and Sam's courage allows them to continue their quest to destroy the ring.

Sam does not only affect Frodo here, but also the whole company. Gandalf has been their clear leader, to this point, but we cannot see, as God can, how the choices of the small affect the great. As already noted, if Gandalf had not survived to face the Balrog, he would not have returned as "Gandalf the White" and the entire future course of the novel would be changed. In this chapter's most famous moment, Gandalf's battle with the Balrog, there is also one of the clearest revelations of the wizard's real nature and purpose. He tells the Balrog, "I am a servant of the Secret Fire, wielder of the flame of Anor. You cannot pass. The dark fire will not avail you, flame of Udûn. Go back to the Shadow! You cannot pass." We don't need to understand the full Thomist metaphysic here, any more than Sam does, to understand that Gandalf's stand is an impenetrable sacrifice that allows the rest of the company to escape to freedom. In biblical terms, Gandalf "lays down his life for his friends," dramatically revealing the love of God at work within Middle-earth.

This recovery of real fire does not seem to lead to the consolation of eucatastrophe within the chapter, but later it does. It is natural for no one to see or feel this, and Sam's wail is the authentic response one should feel. Tolkien himself, according to the recent biography from the learned philologist Raymond Edwards, had paused after writing his way to the tomb of Balin, "baffled" about where the story should go next.[4] This chapter thus becomes the "bridge" not only to the dark place where the Balrog is stopped, and not only to Gandalf's later identity, but also to the growth in Sam that will later be so important to the success of the quest. The sound of drumbeats, the "doom, doom" that closes the chapter seems a dark note, but in the history of English (which Tolkien knew so well), doom refers not mainly to the depressing blows of fate that befall us all, but rather to "doomsday," the final judgement day on which the full justice, truth, and love of God are finally revealed. In Christian tradition, this term normally applies also to the judgement and meeting with God that occurs for every person on their death; is that true also of Gandalf? That is the question that, here, must be resounding in Sam's head.

6. LOTHLÓRIEN: "INSIDE A SONG"

The reality of that hope is certain, and certainly intended by Tolkien, but cannot be felt, here, within the novel's narrative. Aragorn now tells the Company, "We must do without hope," and the reality of their emotional pain means that readers cannot expect to hear much of the comic tone so often important to the hobbits' quest. Yet Aragorn's opening words are so contrary to the book's general philosophy—Tolkien typically gives us very inspiring visions of Hope—that we should also be unsurprised to find in this chapter some of the author's central philosophy, by which he revives both the downcast company and despairing readers. This is the chapter which makes explicit a crucial aspect of Tolkien's Middle-earth that was hinted at before: creation itself, even after the fall of Melkor and all the ensuing conflicts between good and evil, is not entirely fallen, but rather

4. Edwards, *Tolkien*, 192.

retains elements of the Creator's goodness which cannot be erased. In this "old forest" or "loth" of Lórien that they now enter, it is stressed that on this land "there is no stain."

As with Bombadil, unfallen nature seems real, and thus hope can be recovered along the way, in the concrete reality of physical creation such as stone, trees, and, probably most importantly for the novel, light itself. In the light of this forest, we see clearly that Tolkien's Middle-earth is not a place of Manichean struggle between forces of good and evil, but rather part of the Judeo-Christian world in which the fall is not absolute, for many elements of creation retain their original divine blessing. Yet here the company is also told the same thing that Tolkien explains at the start of "On Fairy-Stories": the realm of faërie is "fair and perilous," and it is not easy for mortals to see their way within it. These theological-aesthetical issues are, of course, well beyond anything that would occur to the hobbits, especially to the cheery common sense of Samwise Gamgee, so it is Legolas the Elf who here stands out in the company, much as Gimli did in Moria. Yet the central character in this and the following two chapters, corresponding in importance within the novel to Bombadil and Elrond, is certainly Galadriel the Elf-Queen. Her role in both Tolkien's art and in the narrative journey of the company is thus crucial to understand.

As for Samwise Gamgee, here we see both his concrete realism, and serious interest in Elvish art. Even before entering Lórien, we see Sam "deep in thought" at an example of Elvish beauty particularly valued by Gimli and the dwarves, the reflection of the mountains at the "mirrormere," where the dark mountains of Moria become majestic within the clear waters of the stream that feed the river running through Lórien. Inside the forest, though, where the company joins Elves in sleeping high in the trees, Sam adapts to the unfamiliar as quickly as he did in the House of Tom Bombadil; here also Sam "sleeps like a log," and we wonder why he is different in this respect then the other hobbits. Typically, just before going to sleep Sam is both practical and philosophical, speaking both off the top of his head and from the bottom of his heart, when he asks for quiet or else "I'll drop off, if you take my meaning." Both the literary motif and spiritual meaning here thematically parallel, comically, Gandalf's fall in Moria. However, this becomes no more explicit than it did back when Gandalf is telling Frodo that it might be a hopeful thought to think of Bilbo being "meant" to find the ring. Sam's simple, kind expression, "If you take my meaning," will be repeated often in the novel, here with key words that help us to glimpse the meaning of Lórien.

First, though, the nature of Elvish art, much as Tolkien presents it in "On Fairy-Stories," is shown through the physical recovery that comes as the company walks through the clear stream of Nimrodel, the clean source of both the "mirrormere" and the river that irrigates Lórien. Ancient legends are connected to this stream, inspiring Legolas to poetic song that stands as one of the shining examples of Elvish art in the whole novel. Nimrodel was an ancient "Elven-maid" who herself radiated the light of Ilúvatar:

> A star was bound upon her brows,
> A light was in her hair
> As sun upon the golden boughs
> In Lórien the fair

As the fifteen-stanza song celebrates, though Nimrodel's own life became tragic, marred by evil, the forest itself grew from the light of God that could not be deflected. Sam is almost too physically weak, after Moria, to even cross this stream, to navigate the Elvish bridges which Legolas constructs. Yet later with Frodo he will state perfectly the aesthetic here experienced by both readers and the company: "'It's sunlight and bright day, right enough,' he said. 'I thought that Elves were all for moon and stars: but this is more Elvish than anything I ever heard tell of. I feel as if I was *inside* a song, if you take my meaning.'" The meaning of Sam's colloquial words here becomes clearer: can we partake, at least in part, of the aesthetic beauty that comes from being inside Lórien, a pure realm of beauty, truth, and goodness beyond our capacity to understand?

Answering this question pushes towards the theological issues raised by the nature of art and the person of Galadriel herself, questions so complex that the next chapter is almost entirely devoted to them. Here first we are given an almost allegorical metaphor of how the Company experiences the beauty of fellowship. Dwarves are not normally allowed within Lórien, so at first Gimli is commanded to be blindfolded. Aragorn then decides that the entire company, including Legolas, will travel blindfolded through Lórien. This immense sacrifice accepts darkness, and the loss of created beauty around them, in order to prevent division that might mar the quest. The Elf leading them, Haldir, understands well what they have overcome: "Indeed in nothing is the power of the Dark Lord more clearly shown than in the estrangement that divides all those who will oppose him." Followers of the Gospel today are likely to apply this scene to "the division of Christians against each other."[5]

When the blindfold is lifted, after new commands arrive from Galadriel, it is in both sunlight and the peace of friendship that the entire company then sees "Cerin Amroth," the "heart of the ancient realm as it was long ago." This is not a mythological Eden, for orcs do enter it hunting the fellowship (though none of them will ever exit alive), and as with Bombadil the power of this place is limited. As Tolkien's narrator puts it, "The sun that lay on Lothlórien had no power to enlighten the shadow" that grows outside it. Yet "here in this high place you may see the two powers that are opposed to one another; and ever they strive now in thought, but whereas the light perceives the very heart of the darkness, its own secret has not been discovered." Even "in winter" here "no heart could mourn for summer or for spring. No blemish or sickness or deformity could be seen in anything that grew upon the earth. On the land of Lórien there was no stain."

The "secret" or true nature of Lórien is more broadly revealed in the next chapter, but the conclusion of this chapter focuses again on Aragorn, who first sounded notes of despair after the departure of Gandalf. At the foot of Cerin Amroth, Frodo finds Aragorn "wrapped in some fair memory," and the worries of Time no longer show: "For the grim years were removed from the face of Aragorn, and he seemed clothed in white, a young lord tall and fair; and he spoke words in the Elvish tongue to one whom Frodo could not see. *Arwen vanimelda, namárië!*" Even those who have learnt only the Elvish of the novel can approximate Aragorn's meaning: "Farewell, beautiful Arwen." The last line of the chapter tells us that Aragorn "came there never again a living man," but the marriage of this man and elf will be as important to the conclusion of the third age as Beren and Lúthien were to the First Age. Readers will also understand Aragorn "in white" here better after the return of Gandalf the White, for in both cases the leader is coming back from divine white light that must blind our dim eyes. Aragorn, though, says farewell to a created love with whom he reunites in time, and perhaps that is why this glimpse of eternity is so moving and beautiful. There is, as Aragorn puts it in the chapter's final paragraph, "a light beyond the dark roads that we still must tread." By "still," both Aragorn and Tolkien probably have the older meaning of the word in mind: "always" or "ever."

---

5. Wood, *Gospel*, 130.

7. THE MIRROR OF GALADRIEL: "I SAW A STAR"

The Elvish theological-aesthetic at the heart of both Lórien and Tolkien's art in general is hard to see, harder still to describe. We glimpse the unfallen, but cannot fully describe it because we are far too human, and Elves have long ago departed our world. So how can we see its reality? Hobbits such as Sam are clearly a key part of Tolkien's answer, but in this chapter we come to two further ways to answer this most problematic question. One is the nature of the Lady, Galadriel the Elf-Queen, that the Company begins to feel almost as soon as they enter Lórien, and the second is her "mirror," which can be understood as a complex symbol, as the ring is for evil, for the good of both art and divine revelation. Seeing this as either is aided by the connections between fairy art and divine revelation that Tolkien succinctly states in his epilogue to "On Fairy-Stories," and by understanding the theology which Tolkien's own biography and letters suggest was closest to his heart, but within the chapter there are many intratextual hints of these extratextual insights. There is, as Robert Murray's famous letter to Tolkien well put it, "a positive compatibility" between "the order of Grace," as Catholicism understands it, and the art of Middle-earth.[6]

Within the chapter, this is first suggested when Galadriel gives each member of the company a test, conveyed only by a glimpse, of what their heart truly desires. Readers have been prepared for what this test means, within the novel, in a number of ways. Bombadil, quite plausibly, is unaffected by the ring because he does not have any desires beyond what creation, and hence the Creator, has given. Frodo becomes the ring-bearer at the Council of Elrond, we learned, because Sauron will not be able to see one who has no desire for the power that the ring can give. Later in the novel, Sam uses the ring for good, avoiding orcs and easily giving it back to Frodo, because he has no evil desires for it. So we understand something of the test of Galadriel, as she gazes into the heart of each creature in the company and gives almost a corrective of the despair in which Aragorn opened the previous chapter: "Hope remains while all the company is true."

Sam gives us the fullest account of the nature of this test. As Galadriel looks upon him, he tells the others, "I felt as if I hadn't got nothing on, and I didn't like it. She seemed to be looking inside me and asking me what I would do if she gave me the chance of flying back home to the Shire to a nice little hole with—with a bit of garden of my own." We note the parallel

---

6. Tolkien, *Letters*, 257.

motif of nudity after Bombadil rescued the hobbits from the barrow-wight, and the probable allusion to the unfallen world of Eden, before shame leads to both clothing and hiding from God. Within this chapter, the meaning of Sam's experience is clarified through parallel with the present Company, who all report something similar. This is explained most clearly by the man who will soon fail the test, Boromir. As he puts it, Galadriel "was tempting us, and offering what she pretended to have the power to give." Boromir's skepticism hides a pride which insists he "refused to listen," but the pride of his very human heart will soon be revealed.

For Sam and Frodo, Galadriel's power is further suggested by her "mirror," a pool of water that both hobbits look upon and see visions whose concrete details make them seem real, though the context and coherence of time is not revealed. The "mirror" thus recreates a major medieval literary genre with which Tolkien was very familiar, the "dream vision." Old English poems, such as "The Dream of the Rood," transcended time to reveal the most fundamental theological truths, such as the meaning of Christ's atonement, and became so valued within Anglo-Saxon culture that lines from its poetry were scrawled on lines of precious metal such as the Ruthwell Cross. Sam's vision upon looking into the mirror, though, is deeply disturbing; he must immediately return to the Shire, he feels, because the home of his father, the "old Gaffer," is being destroyed. Experienced readers of the novel recognize this scene from the "scouring of the Shire" that occurs at novel's end, but here Galadriel can only stress that the mirror is not a guide to ethical decision. As we learned from Gildor the Elf when Sam and Frodo were first out of the shire, do not go to the Elves for advice!

But there is more to Galadriel's "mirror." As she says to Sam, her mirror seems an example of the "Elvish magic" that Sam first set out to see, though Galadriel admits that she does not understand exactly what non-Elves "mean" by "magic," and "they seem to use the same word of the deceits of the enemy." The mirror is "dangerous as a guide of deeds," because it is not time-specific. It "shows things that were, and things that are, and things that yet may be." A literary critic may well be reminded here of Aristotle's famous definition of literary *mimesis*, or even of Blake's Bard introducing "Songs of Innocence and Experience," or of many other conceptions of the magic realism of literary art. But what makes Galadriel's mirror so powerful, as with Anglo-Saxon dream vision, is that it reveals realities that do exist, at some time. It is thus an artistic source that builds always on reality that exists already in nature, and thus must be given by a Creator-Artist who truly knows the past, present, and future of creation. Only God qualifies, of course, and if this is understood then it also becomes possible to see the mirror of Galadriel as a complex symbol of the grace given in sacred art, where divine revelation is given shape and form, or beauty.

The mirror is one of the hardest parts of this tale to understand. Craig Bernthal gives another good explanation:

> Through Galadriel's mirror, Frodo and Sam begin to understand they are involved in an immense story, affecting their entire world, going back centuries. They have been given a glimpse of Providence—of the Music of Ilúvatar—and they find that, despite their small stature and humble origins, they have been given critical parts to play, if they will accept. As Gandalf told Frodo at the beginning, "All we have to decide is what to do with the time is given us." Frodo's path is clear even before he looks in the mirror, but the wider consequences of failure are more powerfully brought home.[7]

Galadriel's crucial role in Tolkien's legendarium could be explored in a number of ways, but there is another key scene in this chapter that expands our understanding of her significance. As she tests Frodo, she also reveals that she wears one of the Elven rings, Nenya, whose light allows her to perceive the Dark Lord, and protect Lórien from darkness. When Frodo freely offers her Sauron's ring (itself a sign of her spiritual authority), Galadriel has the same moment of temptation and choice that we saw earlier with Gandalf. She knows that the power of the ring would make her a "beautiful and terrible" queen, but she rejects it. "I pass the test," she explains, accepting that "I will diminish, and go into the West, and remain Galadriel."

Galadriel's humble acceptance of a simple identity is part of the application made in Murray's letter, as he found that Galadriel reminded him of Mary. Tolkien concurred rather than disagreed, even saying that "all my own small perception of beauty" came from Mary.[8] We less spiritual beings can concur, even while understanding that no simple allegory can be affirmed. Galadriel is far too complex a character within Tolkien's legendarium, with a history as long as Gandalf or Bombadil, to be an allegory. Bernthal notes that Galadriel is "one of Tolkien's most complex characters," and traces her both within the legendarium and in extra-textual contexts as

---

7. Bernthal, *Sacramental*, 204.
8. Tolkien, *Letters*, 257.

BOOK TWO

a "Celtic fertility goddess," but he rightly concludes that "only with her final renunciation of the Ring does her character ultimately conform to Mary's."[9]

To put it another way, for Tolkien it is true that Mary is far too significant within "the order of Grace" to be identified with any literary character. Yet within the typology of grace-filled ladies throughout Tolkien's Middle-earth and God's universe, we cannot help but notice the emphasis in Galadriel on free choice, humility, and creative life without the stain of sin. All are key elements of the Marian dogma most controversial within Western Christendom, Mary's Immaculate Conception (not the Virgin Birth of Christ, but rather Mary's own conception without the stain of original sin).

This Marian dogma is directly connected, biologically and providentially, as Catholicism often stresses, to one of the central dogmas which Tolkien's epilogue to "On Fairy-Stories" affirmed as underlying, making possible, hallowing, the happy endings or sudden turn to joy that is aesthetic eucatastrophe: the Incarnation. Mary's paradoxical human role in this dogma, as the Mother of God, is crucial to Catholicism, yet is very often also a source of the division that evinces the power of "the common enemy of mankind" even among faithful Christians, as Tolkien knew so well due to the tragic death of his own mother and tension even in his friendship to C. S. Lewis. Neither this sublime theology nor fraternal controversy, of course, could be understood by Sam. However, this chapter closes with one of the most traditional Marian symbols, often referenced in the Latin words *stella maris*, an image that translates directly into the symbolism of light, in Tolkien's mythology, through the Ainur who forms the Elves from the stars; the Elves of Middle-earth celebrate her, in song, as "Elbereth Gilthonial." On Galadriel's finger, where sits "Nenya" whose light Sauron can neither see nor understand, Sam says, "I see a bright star."

8. FAREWELL TO LÓRIEN: "SOMETHING INAUDIBLE"

The sublime delight that is Lothlórien cannot last forever, if the quest to destroy Sauron's ring is to continue. Celeborn, Fairy-King, begins the chapter by reminding the hobbits of the same concept which led them out of Khazad-dûm and into the forest. "We are come now," he tells them, "to the edge of doom." Again, in Catholic tradition and culture, this word refers both to God's final judgment day, and also to the individual judgement faced by each believer at the end of his or her individual life. The Company

9. Bernthal, *Sacramental*, 196.

have already made their choice, though, and so it is Galadriel who first speaks their answer: "They are all resolved to go forward," she says, "looking in their eyes." But they will not leave as they entered Lothlórien, for the grace of Galadriel changes each member of the company, and they leave with gifts that will be sustaining graces for the journey.

The gifts are both uniquely Elvish and highly practical, reminding us that recovery of the concrete allows consolations both temporal and eternal. "Lembas," Elves' food for a long journey, is often compared to the eucharist because both build the will; the preeminence of the "summit" of sacramental life is a good example, however, of why reading Tolkien as theological allegory is simply silly. Even more practical than "lembas," in Lórien the company is given cloaks that allow them to remain unseen when surrounded by enemies; immensely useful on their dangerous quest, we also note how this gift, unlike Sauron's ring, does not erode individual identity. Very light but sturdy small boats are also given, as the journey will now take them down the river. The Elves also provide the very simple but practical need that Sam had long lamented forgetting: rope. This Elvish rope is made from a unique material, "hithlain," that is both very strong and flexible. These gifts are not simply fantasy, but rather recovery that allows consolation; as the lead Elf succinctly and poetically explains, clearly echoing "On Fairy-Stories": "Leaf and branch, water and stone: they have the hue and beauty of all these things in the twilight of Lórien that we love; for we put the thought of all that we love into all that we make."

Gifts are also given to individual members of the company, with Sam's being typical in that it reflects his deepest desire. Galadriel gives Sam a little box with the rune for G on its lid which could represent her name, "but also it may stand for garden," for it contains earth from her orchard. G is also the first letter, of course, of "Gamgee" and of Sam's nickname for his father, "the old Gaffer." In sum, the rune reminds Sam of the many gifts he has received in his entire life, and from before he is born. When Sam returns to the Shire to face the devastation he saw in Galadriel's mirror, this gift will allow recovery and be a consolation. Even more poignant are the gifts that seem less practical. Gimli asks for nothing, he says, except "a single strand" of Galadriel's hair, "which surpasses the gold of the earth as the stars surpass the gems of the mine." We are most reminded of the ancient, divine sources of Elvish light in Galadriel's gift to Frodo, a "small crystal phial" which has "the light of Eärendil's star," the Silmaril which guided his ship back to Valinor, the eternal home of Tolkien's mythology. This gift, she says, "will be a light to you in dark places," as the darkest moments of the coming journey often show.

Perhaps the greatest gift of all, though, is saved for the end. Galadriel sings in the ancient Elvish language of Quenya, which Tolkien invented as the foundation for the language and names of later periods of Middle-earth, much as Latin serves as the foundation for modern Romance languages. The song "spoke of things little known in Middle-earth," so the hobbits "did not understand the words," yet "as is the way of Elvish words, they remained graven in [their] memory." For the hobbits, and unlearned readers also, Tolkien follows the song with a literal translation, and even an extra sentence explaining that "Varda" is the "Lady whom the Elves in these lands of exile name Elbereth." Tolkien's typology of grace-filled ladies needs no gloss, for the beauty of Galadriel's song does become engraven in our minds. Significantly, the final word in the song, "*namárië*" is the same word of farewell that closed Aragorn's memory of Arwen at Cerin Amroth, at the end of the previous chapter. Galadriel's song is a reminder that there is "a light beyond the dark roads" of time where we must say goodbye to those we love; in the pure beauty of eternal light, we are in the presence of all those who love God.

This "application" perhaps illustrates what Gimli here sees, as they are leaving Lórien, as "the chief peril" of entering the blessed realm of faërie: one never wants to leave it, even if compelled by duty to go on with quests crucial to the triumph of good over evil in the world of time. Galadriel's parting gifts are a reminder that divine graces will be with the company as they continue on their journey; not only the memory but even the living, literal presence of the divine light she shares with them shall be a light in the darkest of places. And in the home whose destruction Sam deeply desires to defend, Galadriel's gift will give a consolation that remains in time for many generations to come, beyond any human plan that Sam, or even Tolkien, could fully imagine.

9. THE GREAT RIVER: "I SAW A LOG WITH EYES!"

After three chapters under the boughs of Galadriel's grace, where the Company would gladly stay, the time comes to move on. The gifts of Galadriel will prove very important to the Company's journey, beginning with the light boats that now let them travel on the river Anduin. An obvious, even clichéd image is thus created: return to the river of Time after a recreative rest in eternity. Tolkien does not shy away from this motif, which clearly parallels the earlier stops in the House of Tom Bombadil and at Rivendell, but instead reinforces that the company's journey is on the river of Time. About midway through the chapter, after Frodo longs for Lórien, "where Galadriel wields the Elven-ring," Aragorn rebukes him by saying:

> Speak no more of it! But so it is Sam: in the land you lost your count. There time flowed swiftly by us, as for the Elves. The old moon passed, and a new moon waxed and waned in the world outside, while we tarried there. And yesterday a new moon came again. Winter is nearly gone. Time flows on to a spring of little hope.

Though the motif is cliché, it works here for two reasons. First, because eternal beauty has been so vivid and alive in Lórien, and second because it is very natural for Aragorn to again feel hopeless faced with the prospect of a long journey without Gandalf. The direct address to Sam (though Frodo has been the previous speaker) perhaps acknowledges Sam's unspoken role as a leader of the company's spirit, courage, and unshakeable hopefulness. New servants of Sauron are in the sky, and the "Nazgûl" seem even more terrifying than the Black Riders. But the graces of Lórien also give new strength. Seeing only shadow in the sky, Legolas cries, "Elbereth Gilthoniel," and his trusty arrow shoots a Nazgûl out of the air!

For his part, Sam seems to share Aragorn's initial return to gloom. Early in the chapter, Sam's interior life is dominated by rational awareness of their present external fears; he "felt that the Company was too naked, afloat in little open boats in the midst of shelterless lands, and on a river that was the frontier of war." Like most hobbits (Merry and the Brandybucks are the exceptions), Sam has little experience in boats; he is too small to effectively row, and often feels useless, as "luggage in a boat." Yet he can also be "luggage with eyes," as Frodo tells him, a watchman on the water whilst the company travels at night, to avoid attention. Yet even in this simple, practical task, Sam's eyes notice two phenomena that should give readers hope along the journey.

Both, however, could inspire further fear if interpreted in a purely physical way unaware of Middle-earth's spiritual past. For the first time since they have set out from the Shire, Frodo and Sam name the strange creature clearly following them—he had been spotted very briefly in the Old Forest, outside Moria, and even in Lothlórien—as Gollum, the infamous contestant of Bilbo for the ring. Here Gollum moves in the shape of a black log along the water, close enough that, as Sam warns, they could suddenly "feel some nasty fingers round our necks." Sam will maintain this commonsensical protectiveness of Frodo throughout their long journey, but he does not yet know he will share this journey with Gollum also! Here, there is only a hint of that journey's spiritual meaning, through a physical detail briefly noticed. Out of the darkness, Gollum cannot help but project also two beams of light, however narrowly slit, that are his eyes.

Experienced readers of the novel are more likely to correctly interpret this detail, though one could here recall Gandalf's words, back in the second chapter of Book I, on Gollum's key role. The less apparent spiritual sign also seen by Sam on the river comes as he exclaims, "Swans! . . . And mighty big ones too!" Sam's excitement is probably that of seeing an extraordinary, beautiful creature of the Shire, so far outside its blessed borders, but readers of Tolkien's legendarium should also see this sign as another of the novel's many types. Eärendil's ship to Valinor, led by the silmaril, was in the shape of a swan; this current company's quest is also headed in the right direction. Aragorn adds an interesting detail, though we wonder how this can be physically seen at night: "They are black swans," he says. Partly Tolkien's point here could be to counter the erroneous identification of white as the color of goodness, and God, while black is the color of the Black Riders, and the growing shadow who is Sauron. That symbolism is grounded in natural light and darkness, but it certainly is not intended to extend to all living creatures. Many other examples within the novel could be given, but an extratextual reference that might well have been important to Tolkien is the "black Madonna" common throughout medieval Europe and also found in England's most important Marian shrine, at Walsingham, whose black Madonna was modeled after the famous "Lady of Loreto" in Italy, itself linked to the Black Madonna at Czestochowa of Poland, held by Catholic tradition to have been first painted by St. Luke.

Extratextual meaning of this kind is impossible to verify, and barely noticed within intratextual reading, but traditional typology, as we have seen, is an essential means by which Tolkien makes the past present. The clearest example of this comes at chapter's end, after the company has been attacked by orcs and is again gripped by fear. Finding themselves in "black waters" that "roared and echoed," Frodo laments, "What a place! What a horrible place!" Then a "strange voice" behind him says, "Fear not!" and turning Frodo no longer sees "Strider," but "Aragorn, son of Arathorn," who repeats, "Fear not!" This type of the King of kings then refers to the

"Argonauth"—the stone carving of ancient kings on cliffs above the river (a visual image that Jackson's film had the funds to reproduce)—to trace his lineage back in time, in order to reassert who he is at present:

> Long have I desired to look upon the likenesses of Isildur and Anarion, my sires of old. Under their shadow Elessar, the Elfstone son of Arathorn of the House of Valandil Isildur's son, heir of Elendil, has nought to dread!

There is reason for fear, however, inside and outside the Company, so here "the light of his eyes faded," and the human leader again speaks in his own voice: "Would that Gandalf were here! How my heart yearns for Minas Andor and the walls of my own city! But wither now shall I go?"

The answer of Aragorn's heart to this difficult question does not become clear until the beginning of Book III, and fear will continue to afflict Frodo in the last chapter of Book II. Here this chapter ends gloomily, with strikingly little creativity, in a very short paragraph meant to convey only that the "tenth day of this journey was over." But the presence of divine providence with them had already been conveyed when, in response, to Aragorn's just stated question, Tolkien's narrator replied, "The chasm was long and dark ahead; but soon Frodo saw a tall gap of light before him, ever growing. Swiftly it drew near, and suddenly the boats shot through, out into a wide clear light."

10. THE BREAKING OF THE FELLOWSHIP: "THINK, IF YOU CAN!"

Seeing the spiritual power pushing the boats along the great river of chapter 9, unglimpsed beneath the black water of fear and uncertainty, is very helpful to noticing a similar pattern in Book II's final chapter. Its initial focus is Frodo going alone to "Amon Hen," which like Weathertop is an ancient lookout built to give advance sight of the enemy. The Black Riders have not yet regrouped since being swept away at the Ford of Bruin, but Frodo is troubled and as unsure of direction as Aragorn; he tries to recall Gandalf's words, but "time went on, and still he was no nearer to a choice."

Suddenly Frodo becomes aware of a new enemy present. Boromir claims to be "afraid" for Frodo, but soon he calmly and rationally explains why it is in everyone's best interest for him to now take the ring. When Frodo flees, aptly asking whether Boromir had listened at all at the Council of Elrond, Boromir realizes he has been "gripped by madness," but the emotion that grips Frodo is fear. Afraid that the ring presents unsurmountable danger for all of the company, Frodo resolves to flee alone, obviously forgetting crucial advice repeatedly given that has allowed the quest to arrive at this point. Elrond's "fellowship" is clearly breaking, but perhaps the title of this chapter is pointing us also, ironically, towards the bond that preceded it?

Sam, we recall, was the "chief investigator" in that conspiracy of friendship, and here again he stands out by alone knowing *exactly* what Frodo is thinking. After noticing Boromir's re-appearance among them and report that Frodo had left with the ring on, Sam quickly draws the correct conclusions: "Mr. Frodo, he knows he's got to find the Crack of Doom. But he's *afraid*." Sam does not know exactly why Frodo has put on the ring, though he suspects Boromir, but he has been there in every previous moment when fear drove Frodo to put on the ring. Yet he also knows that his master and friend will be driven by two other factors: courage, and concern for the other members of the company. So he concludes that Frodo is

> too frightened to start. And he isn't worrying about us either: whether we'll go along with him or no. He knows we mean to. That's another thing that's bothering him. If he screws himself up to go, he'll want to go alone.

Sam's words are colloquial, and realistic rather than sentimental, but Aragorn immediately comments, "I believe you speak more wisely than any of us, Sam."

Aragorn then invites Sam to go with him to search for Frodo, for "none of us should be alone" in this dangerous moment. Aragorn's "heart guessed" that Frodo would go to Amon Hen, but Sam has deeper insight:

> Let me see now! Boromir isn't lying, that's not his way; but he hasn't told us everything. Something scared Mr. Frodo badly. He screwed himself up to the point, sudden. He made up his mind at last—to go. Where to? Off East. Not without Sam? Yes, without even his Sam. That's hard, cruel hard. . . . Think, if you can!

Far from dwelling on personal slight, though, Sam puts to work the less insightful part of him—his head rather than his heart—to quickly deduce that Frodo must have gone first back to the boats. So, "like lightning," or at least as fast as a hobbit can move, Sam follows.

There then occurs one of the great scenes of the book. Bernthal, stressing the sacramental foundations of Tolkien's art, sees it as a type of baptism.[10] Sam does say, "I drownded." Jackson memorably films this scene, following Tolkien's narrative except for one detail: in the novel, as Frodo gets into the boat to begin paddling towards Mordor alone, he puts on the ring, and becomes invisible. In Jackson's film, Elijah Wood, as Frodo, does not put on the ring, making his eyes (always featured by Jackson) even more open windows of his soul as he returns and saves the drowning Sam, who has rushed into the water to follow Frodo even though he can't swim. In either film or novel, the most memorable action is surely Sam wading into the water, even as he speaks of being unable to swim; this willingness to sacrifice his life in turn gives Frodo the opportunity to save Sam, and thus seal the bond of friendship that will carry them through Mordor. As film, Jackson's approach here works very well, and the change from the novel—unlike major blunders such as the omission of Tom Bombadil or the enlargement of the battle of Helm's Deep—can be justified as aesthetic adaptation.

Yet the thematic motifs accentuated by Tolkien's narrative should also be appreciated. To this point in the novel, whenever Frodo puts on the ring, he becomes visible to Sauron's servants, and vulnerable to their attack. Here it is neither clear nor important as to whether Sam sees Frodo or just the moving boat, but certainly Sam knows the real direction of his friend, and knows a love for him so great as to be willing to lay down his own life for his friend. Perhaps here we can pause again and turn to Fleming Rutledge for the biblical verse that theologians typically use to describe Tolkien's development of Sam's relationship to Frodo. Here in this final chapter of Book I:

> Sam the servant thus enters into his destiny, and the first volume ends on a grace note, even as the two Hobbits prepare to descend into Hell. We close our chapter with a biblical recollection. On the night before His own descent into Hell, the Lord Jesus said unto his disciples: "Greater love hath no man, than that he lay down his life for his friends. . . . No longer do I call you servants, for the servant does not know what the master is doing; but I have called you friends" (John 15:13–15).[11]

The simple gardener thus follows in the footsteps of the great Gandalf, and succeeds not by his own strength but by going to a helpless place where Frodo can return to his own soul's deepest longings. As so often in the novel, concrete recovery leads to the consolation of eucatastrophe, though readers

---

10. Bernthal, *Sacramental*, 192–93.
11. Rutledge, *Battle*, 146.

caught by this supremely emotional moment are unlikely to think of such concepts. Rather, they might recall the *namárië* of Gandalf in Moria, or Aragorn at Cerith Amroth, or Galadriel as the company bid farewell to Lorian. Even more wondrous than those "goodbyes," in which an unbreakable spiritual bond remained despite the physical parting, here the hobbits' bond physically overcomes death, and promises to be a friendship that can endure the long road still ahead of them.

Book Four

A EUCATASTROPHIC PLOT TURN

Before focusing directly on Book IV, when we next see Sam with Frodo, it is worth reflecting on Tolkien's decision to divide his major characters and plots for close to the remainder of his long novel; Books III and V stay with Aragorn, Merry, Pippen, and eventually Gandalf (along with a number of fascinating subcreations such as Éowyn or Treebeard), while Books IV and the first few chapters of Book III are mainly devoted to Frodo, Sam, and Gollum, the latter of whom surprisingly becomes a guide to lead all three to Mordor. Why? One could answer in literary terms, as the initial division aids the coherent pursuit of epic romance and diverse adventure, with key minor characters such as Théoden or Saruman, while the second plot allows much more focus upon Sam and the novel's most surprising hobbit, Gollum, as well of course upon the significance of the ring bearer, Frodo. In addition to these literary motives, which are very important to the completion and achievement of such a long project, it is plausible to posit a "two-front war" against Sauron, with Gandalf and Aragorn leading the military battle, while Frodo and Sam pursue the more arduous, and more essential, spiritual war.

However, one should also note the theme of creaturely choice and divine providence that Tolkien develops. In the last chapter of Book IV, Aragorn knows they have come to a "day of choice" for the Company, either to go west to Minas Tirith (Gondor), east to Mordor, or disband. He seems to favor the first option, but once Frodo flees the attack of Boromir, a new, difficult choice must be made: follow Frodo and Sam, or attempt to save Merry and Pippen from the orcs who have captured them. The rational or "missional" choice here is obvious, given that the destruction of the ring is the central purpose for the entire quest, but Aragorn chooses the second option. This might be taken as "hobbit-centric" care for the weak, but many other events occur, beyond hobbit-rescue, as a "side-effect" of this choice, most notably the subsequent meeting with Treebeard (leading to defeat of Saruman) and the reunion with Gandalf the White. Causation is never certain, in literature or life, but certainly the many ways in which the novel's plot brings good out of evil, greater good than anyone could have rationally imagined, must remind us that Providence, or divine action in historical or temporal affairs, is also an essential though rarely perceptible reality within Tolkien's novel and legendarium as a whole.

Tolkien's decision to make divine action implicit rather than explicit, while still intending the sovereignty of God as the central theme of the novel, can make this point difficult to articulate. A colloquial but implicitly Christian description of this decision, one spoken simply within the novel's narrative, are Sam's opening words in Book IV: "Well master, we're in a fix, and no mistake."

To accurately interpret both Sam's and Tolkien's intentions for these words one must avoid a literal, reductionist "translation," and instead adopt the philologist's delight in cognate words and polyvalent meaning.

A literal minded reader will "translate" Sam's words as meaning, "We're in a lot of trouble," but his actual words could suggest much more. "Fix" could mean trouble, but also suggests "preordained plan," as in the modern expression, "the fix was in." "Fix" can also mean, commonly, to mend, or to correct what is broken. The most common historical meaning of the word, though, suggests the opposite of "change," or of current trouble, for historically "fix" most commonly means "place precisely in time or space." Sam's words are right after the final sentence of Book III, which images Gandalf riding with Pippen on Shadowfax, a paradoxically still image of eternity fixed above the changing world of time. This sense of "fix," derived from the Latin word *fixus*, might easily be part of what Tolkien intends by Sam's words, especially given how important the Tridentine Latin Mass was in Tolkien's own spiritual life.

The "good out of evil" motif is also suggested by the word "master," which could refer not only to "Master Frodo," but also every creature's ultimate master, God. As with the word "Lord" in the novel's title, the polyvalent meaning is suggested by the words around it. Finally, "no mistake" could mean "certainly," but also suggests "intention," in much the same way as Gandalf found it comforting to think that Bilbo was "meant" to find the ring. As a "meant" implies a Meaner, so "no mistake" could suggest a

Planner who has not made a mistake in setting Frodo on the path towards Mordor.

1. THE TAMING OF SMÉAGOL: "WE'RE IN A FIX, AND NO MISTAKE"

What one might term "philological" reading can also help, as so often in the novel, with the title of the first chapter in Book IV, "The Taming of Sméagol." Most readers will recognize this as Gollum's original hobbit name, before he took the ring by murdering his friend Deagol after the two were fishing together. "Sméagol" is a name we have not heard since Gandalf's account of this crime back in "The Shadow of the Past," and even there Gandalf mentions "Sméagol's grandmother" while normally calling him "Gollum." Within this chapter, a sympathetic Frodo will often use the name Sméagol, and directly recall the key passage where Gandalf urged pity and said that Sméagol yet might have "some good to do in the lives of many." Yet Sam and the narrator normally call him "Gollum," and Sam reminds us of the origin of this name, the muffled sound made when the alienated, murderous hobbit turned away from his neighbors, by growling, "I'll give him gollum in the throat."

Theological interpreters rightly stress the *imago Dei* in Sméagol, but Sam's treatment of Gollum is not simply hard-heartedness, though the journey to Mordor is so stressful that even Sam himself is unaware of "the dark cloud settling on his heart." If Sam had not been wary and distrustful of Gollum, it is doubtful that either he or Frodo would ever have reached Mount Doom, or that the ring itself would ever have been destroyed. Therefore both Frodo's and Sam's treatment of their sad, elder fellow hobbit must be taken as part of the providential plan suggested by Gandalf. "Even the wise cannot see all ends," the great *maiar* rightly said, and so we should not be surprised when, early in the chapter, Frodo wonders whether "good or evil" will show the path to Mordor. As Tolkien stresses in "Ainulindalë," the creation account of *The Silmarillion*, it is a key aspect of providence that God can use both.

Precise diction is also important in the other key word in the title of the crucial opening chapter of Book IV. "Taming" is a very old English word still commonly used, though modern readers might assume that it simply refers to how the formerly wild pursuer of the ring now becomes an aid to Frodo's journey. But this sense most clearly refers to Gollum, whereas

BOOK FOUR

the syntax of the title demands us to apply it to Sméagol. Here older, cognate senses of "tame" can help us, as Tolkien himself would have found in translating *Sir Gawain and the Green Knight*. Near the conclusion of that Middle English masterpiece, we hear how at least part of the Green Knight's enchantment came through "Morgan the Goddess," against whom "none power and pride possess / too high for her to tame." "Taming" in the title of chapter 1 of Book IV is not an allusion to Gawain. It is, however, a reminder that "tame," historically, could mean the mastering of the sin passed on to all creatures, pride being the most universal. Shakespeareans will here think of *The Taming of the Shrew*, but Tolkien's genre is not a farce of human nature. The chapter title here is "The Taming of Sméagol," not Gollum, and much depends, especially in Book IV, on this distinction. Perhaps what Frodo and Sam must really attempt in this book is not the control of the wild beast "Gollum," but a far more difficult attempt to help "Sméagol" overcome the self-centered pride that first led him to murder because, as Sméagol put it *before* being corrupted by the ring, "It's my birthday."

However important it is to the narrative, an absolute contrast between "good Sméagol" and "evil Gollum" is as inaccurate as seeing the whole of the novel as a battle between good and evil. As one cannot be reminded too often, the novel is not Manichean, about the clash between material good and evil, however real both seem at various moments, but rather the Augustinian clash between eternal divine reality and the illusory shadow of evil. The challenge of overcoming "power and pride" in Sméagol becomes part of why Frodo comes to sympathize with him; it is the burden of the ring. Sam is right to monitor the shadow of Gollum, which must haunt them as they travel in time, on the way to destroy the ring. God's providence, above the terrifying reality of the Nazgûl (the Black Riders now not on horseback but flying about on some dragon-like creature) or Sauron's eye, is guiding them even as it seems "they were now wholly in the hands of Gollum." Being in the "hands of God" is an almost clichéd term for divine providence, but Tolkien show its reality through inference rather than reference.

Sam's colloquial philology, calling Sméagol "slinker" and Gollum "stinker," might seem initially too simple to be relevant thematically except as comic relief; as, for example, when Sam calls himself a "ninyhammer," recalling that as "a word" of his "Gaffer," his term of endearment for his Father. At the end of this same sentence, punctuated as a single sentence, is the single simple word for the key concrete object of the chapter: "Rope." Initially in the chapter, even Sam seems to be tiring of the Elvish, longing for "a bit of plain bread, and a mug—aye, half a mug—of beer" instead of *lembas*. But, as he and Frodo face the practical challenge of descending the Emyn Muil, "rope" becomes practically essential, and its Elvish character helps he and Frodo not only to descend but, as is normative for Tolkien's philology, to recover the *real* meaning of this word.

Much more than an efficient tool that Frodo first says they are "lucky" to have along, a common misnaming of providence, this rope is an Elvish product of the highest virtue. Sam recognizes this in recalling how the rope came into their Elven boats on leaving Lórien, when Haldir the Elf said, "It may be a help in many needs." More solemnly, Sam thinks the rope "made by Galadriel herself, too, maybe," and, repeating her name, he "murmured, nodding his head mournfully."

As Frodo and Sam descend, the Elvish character of the rope is shown in two further ways: it "shimmers" or glows in the dark, and seems to break its knot when Sam calls, or at least Sam thinks that the most likely explanation of how one of his expert knots breaks. Frodo is less certain, but for him the rope literally becomes the "light in the dark" that Galadriel had promised her gifts would be. He has been fully blind during their descent, a foreshadowing early in the novel of his full dependence on both his friends and God, but the rope returning to Sam causes Frodo to recover his sight; aware now of the great blessing that so many take for granted, Frodo says:

> "It's good to be able to see again," said Frodo, breathing deep. "Do you know, I thought for a bit that I had lost my sight? From the lightning or something else worse. I could see nothing, nothing at all, until the grey rope came down. It seemed to shimmer somehow."

But perhaps the most important word in the chapter is the one highlighted here by Tolkien through italics, reprinting the crucial conversation between Frodo and Gandalf first given us back in chapter 2: *pity*. Presented as the ongoing mental presence of Gandalf, as Frodo heard him at the end of Book I, here as earlier we hear this key perspective on Gollum:

> *What a pity Bilbo did not stab the vile creature, when he had a chance!*
> *Pity? It was Pity that stayed his hand. Pity, and Mercy: not to strike without need.*
> *I do not feel any pity for Gollum. He deserves death.*
> *Deserves death! I daresay he does. Many that live deserve death. And some die that deserve life. Can you give that to them? Then be*

> *not too eager to deal out death in the name of justice, fearing for your own safety. Even the wise cannot see all ends.*

Frodo concludes, here at the start of Book IV, "Now that I see him. I do pity him."

Wood is absolutely correct when he argues that "nowhere is *The Lord of the Rings* made more manifestly Christian than in its privileging of pity—mercy and forgiveness—as its central virtue."[1] Though "pity" is another of the modern words emptied of meaning by trivial misapplication, Tolkien knows its historical, theological significance, if not in many other sources, from *Sir Gawain and the Green Knight*. "Pitié," the French word and Middle English equivalent of "pity," is one of the five virtues linked interdependently in the pentangle, the symbol on Gawain's shield. Arguably, "pitié," is the most important of the five virtues, it being why the Green Knight laughs at Gawain for hiding the green garter that he imagines saves his life, and why the knights of the Round Table welcome him back despite the young Gawain's own self-condemnation for lack of courage. Though entertained readers can easily miss the main point, as many readers of *The Lord of the Rings* also miss this point, the pity shown to Gawain can ultimately be meaningful only because of the pity shown creation by the Creator in the Incarnation and all that it allowed. As argued in chapter 2 of Book I, meaning requires a Meaner. "Pity" is thus linked in an essential way to "eucatastrophe," and recovering its meaning is thus also essential to understanding the larger consolation offered by Tolkien's great novel.

Alongside such sublime concepts, Sam can seem very small. Yet the chapter often suggests, if only by negative inference, Sam's essential presence on the journey. At the end of the chapter, Frodo forces Gollum to swear not "on" but "by" the Precious, and we may be confused by the distinction. Yet as Sam looks on the more essential philological point is made; the "Precious" is imagined by Gollum to be the ring, and we know that this word also functions as a synonym for Gollum's own identity, which he is no longer capable of distinguishing from the ring. Yet Sméagol is a soul as precious to God as any, including Frodo, Gawain, or any historical being. It is thus God as Master whom Gollum will swear by and serve on the journey, even as he himself does not understand this in promising, "I will serve the master of the Precious. Good master, good Sméagol." After hearing this, Sam demonstrates the meaning of true servanthood by obeying Frodo and letting Gollum off the rope (which like all things Elvish burns sin), which

1. Wood, *Gospel*, 149.

has to be against Sam's rational judgement. The three hobbits then begin walking towards Mordor in the black of night. They are also "under hard clear stars," and this Elvish, divine light will show them the way, even, in the words of the chapter's conclusion, in "black silence."

2. THE PASSAGE OF THE MARSHES: "WHERE'S THAT DRATTED CREATURE?"

The key point inferred often in chapter 1, that Sméagol is both a hobbit like Frodo and that Gollum is a hardened sinner very different than Sam, is repeated memorably at the start of chapter 2. First the wayward, ancient hobbit gives us poetry, and then where one would rhyme "fish," he remembers the exact words used in *The Hobbit* in the riddle contest with Bilbo. Sam also recalls this encounter as he has the chance to kill a sleeping Gollum after this creative outburst, the crucial chance that Bilbo also declined before his memorable "leap in the dark." Perhaps unaware of how important his likeness is here to Bilbo, Sam instead comments on difference: "If I was like Gollum, he wouldn't never wake up again." One respects the emotion that causes Sam to protect his master, but we also delight in how Sméagol/Gollum, in his own poetic words, can "bless us and splash us."

Adding a third travel companion does raise, however, a practical problem with which Sam is very often concerned in Book IV: food. Sam well remembers, and Tolkien never lets us forget, that Gollum's prize in *The Hobbit* "riddle contest" was to eat Bilbo. Sam's concern for food leads to one of the oft-quoted examples of the "northern theory of courage," the courage to fight even when the fight is unwinnable, as Frodo reminds Sam that they are probably not going to need food for a return journey. Sam's response is mainly non-verbal, but deeply meaningful:

> Sam nodded silently. He took his master's hand and bent over it. He did not kiss it, though his tears fell on it. Then he turned away, drew his sleeve over his nose, and got up, and stamped about, trying to whistle, and saying between the efforts: "Where's that dratted creature?"

Sméagol is a "creature," and for Sam or anyone else to call him that is a reminder that he has a Creator. Sméagol, at least for the moment, seems more real than "Gollum," faithfully leading Sam and Frodo through smelly marshes so disgusting that even the orcs don't want to travel this way. These marshes might seem a paradoxical form of "holy water," but Tolkien complicates any Catholic "application" here even more through the "candles of corpses" inside each marsh, which seem to represent long dead soldiers in from the great war between Sauron and Isildur that closed the second age. On the face of it, to use a phrase that here comes to mind, this seems an obvious allusion to one of the most commonplace and distinctive practices of Catholic piety, the lighting of candles in prayer for dead souls. Except of course that the dead here must be illusory, a physical phantasm, and, as so often with Tolkien, allegory is simply a fruitless error. Gollum tested this by trying and failing to "touch" (probably steal from) these phantasms, and it seems to be simple common sense when Sam comments, "The Dead can't be really there! Is it some devilry hatched in the Dark Land?"

The answer to Sam's question is "probably," though as with Gawain one can't be sure of the true source of the magic. Perhaps God, who always brings good out of evil, intends the "candles of corpses" to function like a medieval *memento mori*, which can depress one into hell or remind the soul of eternal life. The deeper and much more important Catholic motif here concerns the will, both how the Dark Lord tries to take over one's will and how our Good Lord works against this. We often heard this theme when Frodo first began bearing the ring, but in the land of Mordor this burden is magnified as he moves closer to Sauron:

> With every step towards the gates of Mordor, Frodo felt the Ring on its chain about his neck grow more burdensome. He was now beginning to feel it as an actual weight dragging him earthwards. But far more he was troubled by the Eye: so he called it to himself. It was that more than the drag of the Ring that made him cower and stoop as he walked. The Eye: that horrible growing sense of a hostile will that strove with great power to pierce all shadows of cloud, and earth, and flesh, and to see you: to pin you under its deadly gaze, naked, immovable.

Against the hostile will of Sauron there is the steady presence of Sam's friendship, and here Sam alters the order of their procession, which had moved, in order, Gollum, Sam, Frodo, so that Sam "put Frodo in front of him now," and was "trying to encourage him with clumsy words."

The yet deeper Catholic motif here, as throughout the novel, is the providence of God. There are traces of God's presence even in Mordor, as we shall notice. For Sam and Frodo, though, this presence is almost known by absence, as in the dark path of the *via negativa* mystics, for this is "a land defiled, diseased beyond all healing—unless the Great Sea should enter in and wash it with oblivion." Here is the famous image of God that Dante famously connects, with the help of Piccarda the nun in paradise, to the need the human will has for the divine will; in Longfellow's translation, "His will is our peace: this is the sea / To which is moving onward whatsoever / It doth create, and all that nature makes."[2]

Frodo's path is leading into eternity, but it is Sam's duty to help his Master in time, which he here does by pretending to sleep and overhearing an interior dialogue, a *psychomachia*, in which Sméagol and Gollum argue about the path each wants to follow. Neither wants "He," Sauron, to get the ring, but Sam is disturbed to not know who "She" is who might yet aid recovery of the ring. Pretending to sleepily wake up—asking, "What's the time?"—Sam and Sméagol/Gollum soon agree that it is "high time" for them to continue, but Frodo has been touched by a different spirit in sleep: "Frodo awoke refreshed. He had been dreaming. The dark shadow had passed, and a fair vision had visited him in the land of disease. Nothing remained of it in his memory, yet because of it he felt glad and lighter of heart."

Somehow, divine peace is still present even in this place, and the chapter's conclusion suggests further traces of the Trinity even in evil, as "three times" the Nazgûl fly close, and Sméagol/Gollum gives another interpretation that reminds us that Sauron is master of the ring but God is the Master of all: "Three times is a threat. They feel us here, they feel the Precious. The Precious is their master." Physically, the three hobbits here are just "squeaking ghosts" as the chapter's final sentence tells us that they "walked in silence, with bowed heads, seeing nothing, and hearing nothing, but the wind hissing in their ears." Yet "nothing" here does not mean nihilism, but rather the holy absence that paradoxically points to divine presence (see 2 Cor 6:10). Neither is the wind meaningless, for it is one of Christ's favorite images of the Holy Spirit (see John 3:8).

3. THE BLACK GATE IS CLOSED: "BEYOND ANY GAMGEE TO GUESS"

As this chapter opens, the hopelessness of the journey is again stressed. The three hobbits are now in Mordor, and as they come closer to the main entrance to Sauron's kingdom, the Black Gate, the need for "northern

2. Alighieri, *Divine Comedy*, 502.

courage" becomes even more apparent. As usual Sam puts this in the plainest of terms, "Here's the Gate, and it looks to me as if that's about as far as we are ever going to get," but then his thoughts turn to his father. Rather than simple lament, Sam laughs at how his father will "miss his chance of *I told'ee so, Sam*." Yet it is both heartfelt and practical when Sam immediately adds: "He could go on telling me as long as he'd got breath, if only I could see his old face again. But I'd have to get a wash first, or he wouldn't know me." Not even water to wash is readily available in Mordor, however, and there seems to be even fewer sources of hope. Sam does not know what Frodo now should do, and he humbly admits that "it's beyond any Gamgee to guess what he'll do next." Frodo himself is perplexed, and possibly even Tolkien himself; certainly, these are not merely rhetorical questions when the narrator asks, "Which way should he choose? And if both led to terror and death, what good lay in choice."

Hopelessness and uncertainty makes Frodo's courage in front of the Black Gate, the constructed entrance to Sauron's kingdom, even more impressive: "I am commanded to go to the land of Mordor, and therefore I shall go. . . . If there is only one way, then I must take it. What comes after must come." Sam's response shows the perhaps even greater courage of the servant, obedient to his master even unto death:

> Sam said nothing. The look on Frodo's face was enough for him; he knew that words of his were useless. And after all he never had any real hope in the affair from the beginning; but being a cheerful hobbit he had not needed hope, as long as despair could be postponed. Now they were come to the bitter end. But he had stuck to his master all the way; that was what he had chiefly come for, and he would still stick to him. His master would not go to Mordor alone. Sam would go with him—and at any rate they would get rid of Gollum.

Sam does not speak here, but this is a key passage for understanding his nature: neither Sam's habitual cheerfulness nor firm commitment to Frodo is grounded in exterior words, even abstract concepts such as "hope," nor interior feelings that are subject to mood changes. Rather, it is that faculty of the soul traditionally called the "will" that sustains him. His intellect clearly cannot guide Frodo, and he is quite mistaken about Gollum leaving anytime soon, but his will to serve Frodo will not change.

For once, Gollum seems to be speaking some truth, accurately describing entrance to the Black Gate as surrender to Sauron, and accurately describing "another way" further south where he once travelled. Sam is surely right to remain wary of Gollum, as is probably right that there is a "temporary alliance" between "Slinker" and "Stinker" to avoid their common enemy from getting the ring. But it is a more specific truth that Frodo speaks to in accepting the plan of "Sméagol":

> I will trust you once more. Indeed it seems that I must do so, and that it is my fate to receive help from you, where I least looked for it, and your fate to help me whom you long pursued with evil purpose. So far you have deserved well of me and have kept your promise truly.

Grateful for this praise, Gollum seems to take it as a compliment to his native hobbit courage: "Sméagol's bones shake to think of it, but he doesn't run away." But then Frodo prophetically clarifies the precise moment of danger that he speaks of:

> I did not mean the danger that we all share.... In the last need, Sméagol, I should put on the Precious; and the Precious mastered you long ago. If I, wearing it, were to command you, you would obey, even if it were to leap from a precipice or to cast yourself into the fire. And such would be my command. So have a care, Sméagol!

This apparent allusion to the yet to come events of Mount Doom suggests God's foreknowledge and providence, but on a strictly natural level Frodo's tone impresses Sam because he had always seen the confusion of "kindness and blindness" as Frodo's one failing, despite Sam also holding "the incompatible belief that Mr. Frodo was the wisest person in the world (with the possible exception of Old Mr. Bilbo and of Gandalf)."

The obvious contradiction here allows a rare comical moment in this angst-ridden chapter, but what really changes the tone is when Sam steps forward, "putting his hands behind his back (as he always did in 'speaking poetry')." The poem is directly sparked by honest, hobbitish questions from Gollum—"What are oliphaunts?"—but the form of the poem serves to more directly put Sam in the riddling tradition of Bilbo and Gollum. Sam starts with a rhyming riddle, "Grey as a mouse / Big as a house," and breaks the rhyme only to give the answer, before adding more rhymes on the Oliphaunt. He comments, "That is a rhyme we have in the Shire. Nonsense maybe, and maybe not." Sam knows that poetry cannot simply be dismissed as non-historical, even if he has not yet seen the poetic subject.

BOOK FOUR

Certainly the poem is not without significance. In darkness of mind, Gollum reverts to a subjectivism that slides quickly towards nihilism, "No, no oliphaunts. . . . Sméagol has not heard of them. He does not want them to see them. He does not want them to be." Frodo, though, "laughed in the midst of all his cares," and this laughter "released him from hesitation." This loss of anxiety finally allows Frodo's actions to mirror his intellect so that he can follow Gollum away from the black gate. This action could be seen as error, given the evil "She" who awaits there, but also as yet another instance in the novel when good is brought out of evil, as the way does finally allow entry to Mount Doom. Again, Sam's comic words seem like nonsense, but allow, ultimately, divine sense to be known.

4. OF HERBS AND STEWED RABBIT: "WHAT A LIFE!"

As Sam and Frodo follow Gollum on "another way" out of Mordor, they enter "Ithilien," a land much healthier, fertile, and flowing with streams that has long been regarded as "the flower of Gondor," but now is controlled by men loyal to Sauron. Rather than political considerations, the much more practical issue of food is again on the hobbits' mind, and again Gollum and Sam contrast each other in comical ways, yet their roles also seem complimentary on the broader providential path that Frodo is following.

Sméagol tells us that "he's very hungry, yes, Gollum!" So the two identities are clearly present in his own mind, and when we see "a pale green light come into his eyes," Sam's mistrust seems again wise. Food is also on Sam's mind, and the more fertile landscape reminds him of the Shire, and his favorite food there. Sam's desire is enough for him to enlist Gollum to go catch "coney," or rabbits, and he even calls him his original name (for the only time in the novel), in asking for the delicacy that flavors the cooking and finds its way into our chapter title: "Be good Sméagol and fetch me the herbs, and I'll think better of you." Gollum's preference, however, is raw rabbit, and as Sam's determination to cook the "coney" he must revert to threat to enlist Gollum's aid, and eventually such threats are simply ignored and Sam "in the end had to find what he wanted for himself."

Yet this chapter is far more than comical interplay over food. While Gollum is away hunting, Frodo sleeps; as Sam looks at him, Frodo's transcendent spiritual nature shines through:

> Sam looked at him. The early daylight was only just creeping down into the shadows under the trees, but he saw his master's face very

clearly, and his hands, too, lying at rest on the ground beside him. He was reminded suddenly of Frodo as he had lain, asleep in the house of Elrond, after his deadly wound. Then as he had kept watch Sam had noticed that at times a light seemed to be shining faintly within; but now the light was even clearer and stronger. Frodo's face was peaceful, the marks of fear and care had left it; but it looked old, old and beautiful, as if the chiseling of the shaping years was now revealed in many fine lines that had before been hidden, though the identity of the face was not changed.

Such thoughts are Tolkien's narrator, not Sam Gamgee's, but the entire passage does seem a way to remind us, in the middle of the practically necessary task of hunting for food, of "the workings of a transcendent dimension."[3] As so often in the novel, it is through Sam's eyes that Tolkien shows us this dimension.

Sam's flaws also teach here, however; we must say that Gollum is correct to warn against starting a fire to cook for "it will bring enemies." Shortly thereafter, Frodo also chides Sam, saying that "lighting a fire was dangerous in these parts," and it is just after Sam himself notices smoke from the cooking fire that the hobbits are captured by men of Gondor who have spotted the fire. Yet the leader of these men, Faramir, will prove to be one of the most virtuous and important characters in the entire novel. He and his men have come looking for Gollum, confused "what kind of thing it is," but upon capturing Frodo and Sam they have their first introduction to hobbits, and are amazed by the "half-lings" knowledge of their own Gondor legends of the "sword-half broken." Later we learn that Faramir is the brother of Boromir, but even before we learn this he asks the crucial question of the ring—"What is Isildur's bane?"—that drives Frodo and Sam's entire quest. So the error seems somewhat analogous to Pippen's fateful toss of the stone down the well in Moria; Faramir is much less fearsome than the Balrog, of course, but in both cases someone who seems evil actually leads to great good.

Discernment of Faramir's nature dominates the next few chapters of Book IV, but in this seemingly trivial chapter we see again the pattern of relationship between the three hobbits. Sam's mistrust of Gollum and apparent lack of care for Sméagol, which here clearly crosses to a point where readers must admit error or even unethical selfishness, leads to a reaction from Gollum and Frodo that seems justified rebuke. Yet in this very error,

---

3. Rutledge, *Battle*, 212.

in the natural desire that Sam has to cook food which can sustain his master, the actions of Sam turn the plot towards a path that leads to the many eucatastrophes of Book VI. We will have much more to say about Faramir in the coming chapters, but even here his appearance as a "man in green" links him to the Green Knight who, as Tolkien seems to allude especially in the first few chapters of Book IV, tests the poem's hero in ways that readers cannot be sure to deem magical enchantment or divine providence. Their "captain's life is charmed," Faramir's men maintain, for "fate spares him for some other end." This soldier has the commonplace misnaming of providence as "fate," but it is much more traditional Catholic diction that Frodo finally uses to declare friendship with Faramir: "I am a friend of all enemies of the One Enemy."

So common is this reference to the "common enemy of man"[4] as Macbeth terms Satan, that this meeting becomes applicable not only to the spiritual war inside of *The Lord of the Rings* but almost directly applicable to the spiritual warfare that Catholicism regards as fundamental to human life. As a devout Catholic, Tolkien could not have failed to note this application, nor failed to employ it as part of his "mixed marriage" to Edith in which ecumenism had to be necessary but difficult. Frodo's declaration of friendship goes far beyond this moment of the novel, linking its motifs to the "faint echoes of *evangelium*" that Tolkien's "On Fairy-Stories" tells us come from enchanted art.

Frodo's great maxim is surely one of the most significant *sententia* of the novel, but it's also highly interesting that Tolkien places it in the middle of the chapter and instead concludes with perspectives of Sam that can seem childish, if not trivial. The first, Sam's "first view of human war," takes up a subject that can rightly be understood as the common outcome of the inverse of Frodo's great principle, in which the One Enemy turns all men into enemies. Sam's simple response to it, that "he did not like it much," can also seem banal and uninteresting. But then arrows fell a soldier dead near Sam's side, and though glad, as anyone but especially children would be, that he cannot see the dead man's face, Tolkien's narrator gives Sam thoughts that must occur to any humane soldier: "He wondered what the man's name was and where he came from; and if he was really evil of heart, or what lies or threats led him on the long march from his home; and if he would not really rather have stayed there in peace."

---

4. Shakespeare, *Macbeth*, 3.1.70.

RECOVERING CONSOLATION

An even more childish subject for Sam closes the chapter, however: an "oliphaunt." The legendary subject of Sam's riddle-poem at the end of the previous chapter suddenly comes to life as an elephant carrying the Southern men whom the men of Gondor are ambushing is spooked and careens out of control in Sam's direction. Any simple attempt to claim this beast as obvious evidence that Middle-earth is our earth, or even that the "oliphaunt" is an elephant before the "great vowel shift" that Tolkien and all philologists are well aware happens after Middle English, is rejected by the narrator, for though "the Mumak of Harad was indeed a beast of vast bulk," yet "the like of him does not walk now in Middle-earth," and "his kin that live still in latter days are but memories of his girth and majesty." Neither scholarly nor fearful, Sam's reaction to the Mumak is instead the one we have seen before with Elves or other creatures seldom seen in the Shire: delight. "What a life," Sam exclaims, conscious again that for all the hardships of this journey, he is being given the opportunity to see the wonders of our Creator. Again, Sam's "childish" perspective recovers something of the consolation awaiting us in the kingdom of heaven.

5. THE WINDOW ON THE WEST: "THAT WAS GOOD AND TRUE"

The title of the chapter directly refers to the natural wonder revealed at its end, but the more important subject is Faramir himself, who by his historical knowledge and, above all, integrity of character, gives the hobbits, and readers, a living window into the nature of the men of the West, from whom Gondor descends. Sam might seem an unimportant figure in this whole story, but again Tolkien makes him central, first as an observer to how Faramir and Frodo interact. No one notices as Sam awakes, and creeps to "where he could see and hear all that was going on." Faramir continues the questions he has for Frodo upon first meeting him, and "Sam soon became aware that the Captain was not satisfied with himself at several points." Most of all, regarding "Isildur's bane," the ring, from which Faramir has deduced that "Frodo was concealing from him some matter of great importance."

Sam soon becomes irritated with Faramir's suspicious questions, and boldly strides in front of the assembled soldiers and prisoners, saying "this has gone on long enough," addressing Faramir as though he were "a young hobbit who had offered him what he called 'sauce' when questioned about visits to the orchard." Readers are reminded of Sam's mistrust of Strider, about whom Sam was clearly in error, even if his heart was in the right place in defending his master. Just as in that case, Faramir immediately gives sign of noble character, responding to Sam "without anger" but more amusement. Yet Faramir, like Aragorn, is a man of principle and ethics, whose questions have been seeking truth rather than any malicious motive; "I would not snare even an orc with a falsehood," he pledges to Frodo.

Faramir fulfills this pledge as fully, for the novel as a whole, as Aragorn. His role as a man who can truly love Éowyn, developed in Book VI, is almost as important (and therefore almost as understated), as Aragorn's love of Arwen or Sam's love of Rosie. Failure to understand or appreciate Faramir's role is one of the main failings of Peter Jackson's films, which often portray Tolkien's main characters accurately, because Jackson makes Faramir act similarly to Boromir, arresting the hobbits and bringing them to Gondor. In the novel, however, it is precisely the fear that Faramir will act as Boromir which causes Sam and Frodo to worry.

When Faramir does the opposite, however, it is an important reminder that the moral choices of human beings, like hobbits, are not entirely determined by the fate of one's birth; one also has a will, and memory, and intellect, to guide choice. Faramir uses all three here to learn the truth from Frodo, and eventually proves, as much as Aragorn, to be a man driven by the will to love—love of his country, king, and even family (however troubled we know his brother and father to be)—and a man whom even half-wise Sam can trust.

As Frodo and Faramir talk, and this smart, sensitive man gets ever closer to the truth, Sam again is put in the mode of observer, and "had taken no part in the conversation," yet this exceptionally sensitive hobbit "had listened," and even "caught a brief glimpse of a small dark shape slipping behind a tree trunk." Wherever Gollum is, his dark presence is suggested just before Faramir leads Frodo and Sam to a waterfall that he calls "the Window of the Sunset, Henneth Annûn, fairest of all the falls of Ithilien, land of many fountains." It faces West, and serves as a physical way to turn to and remember the Númenor where, in the second age, the Kingdom of Men gloriously stood. It is perhaps apt even to call the falls sacramental, for the next morning Faramir leads the hobbits in one of the very few moments of religious ritual that Tolkien's edits did not excise. Before eating, Faramir "faced west in a moment of silence," and tells them:

RECOVERING CONSOLATION

"We look toward Númenor that was, and beyond to Elvenhome that is, and to that which is beyond Elvenhome and will ever be."

Frodo leads a reverent bow in response, but Sam again says nothing. We know he is awake, though, because he had pledged to do so during the long night before, and even "stuck his knuckles in his eyes," and when a washbowl is brought to him the next morning, "to the astonishment and amusement of the Men he plunged his head into the cold water and splashed his neck and ears." Sam explains with a gardener's metaphor: "if you're short of sleep cold water on the neck's like rain on a wilted lettuce." Sam is so invigorated that after Faramir tells them more on the history of the West—including the crucial fact that the Númenoreans "lost their kingdom" because they could not accept the gift of death, and "hungered after endless life unchanging"—Sam bursts into one of the novel's longest praise of Galadriel, that representative of Elvish holiness that is so important to the connection between Tolkien's faith and fairyland:

> "The Lady of Lórien! Galadriel!" cried Sam. "You should see her indeed you should, sir. I am only a hobbit, and gardening's my job at home, sir, if you understand me, and I'm not much good at poetry—not at making it: a bit of a comic rhyme, perhaps, now and again, you know, but not real poetry—so I can't tell you what I mean. It ought to be sung. You'd have to get Strider, Aragorn that is, or old Mr. Bilbo, for that. But I wish I could make a song about her. Beautiful she is, sir! Lovely! Sometimes like a great tree in flower, sometimes like a white daffadowndilly, small and slender like. Hard as di'monds, soft as moonlight. Warm as sunlight, cold as frost in the stars. Proud and far-off as a snow-mountain, and as merry as any lass I ever saw with daisies in her hair in springtime. But that's a lot o' nonsense, and all wide of my mark."

Sam struggles for poetic metaphor, but clearly understands Galadriel's significance, as he especially shows when Faramir describes her as "perilously fair"; "I don't know about *perilous*," Sam answers, explaining that the real peril lies with those who bring their own perils before her. Though in colloquial rather than theological language, this seems to be an excellent way to understand why sin recoils from the presence of holiness, as we have seen Gollum recoil from all things Elvish. Frodo is "aghast," and it seems Sam has made another major error. For a moment Faramir seems dangerous, understanding Boromir's temptation and with "a strange smile," standing up and exclaiming, "A chance for Faramir Captain of Gondor, to show his quality! Ha!" Readers are reminded very much of the moments when Gandalf and Galadriel are tempted to take the ring, but like them Faramir sits down and begins "to laugh quietly," before recalling that firm moral principle he had told Frodo: "Not if I found it on the highway would I take it."

Faramir even explains to Sam the principle of good being brought out of evil, so important to Tolkien's conception of Ilúvatar, and to the role played anywhere by error in God's creation, by telling Sam: "Strange though it may seem, it was safe to declare this to me. It may even help the master that you love. It shall turn to his good, if it is in my power." For his part Sam's mistrust of Faramir is entirely gone, and he gives perhaps the greatest compliment to men in the novel by saying that Faramir "showed your quality, the very highest," giving "an air" that even reminded Sam of "well, Gandalf, of wizards." To which this most humble, unusual man references again his heritage: "Maybe you discern from far away the air of Númenor. Good night!" Again, we discern with wonder at how Sam has perceived "the true spiritual home 'far away' of all the Men who fight for Middle-earth."[5]

6. THE FORBIDDEN POOL: "CHILLY TO THE HEART"

After Sam has played such a leading role in discerning the character of both Faramir and Gollum, it is unsurprising that in this chapter Tolkien focuses instead on Frodo. Sam has perhaps his fewest lines in all the novel. Gollum has found the pool below the "waterfall," in violation of Gondor law; in fact, his life is "forfeit" just for viewing the pool without permission, let alone swimming or catching fish in it. More clearly than anywhere else in the novel, Frodo here acts as a "Christ figure," in literally saving Gollum from death by law, even as this sinner rejects the means of salvation, for Frodo must lead Gollum back to Faramir and thus seem treacherous. Nowhere is Gandalf's call for pity for Gollum more directly practiced, as Frodo explains to Faramir that "this creature is in some way bound up with my errand" and was even his "guide." Faramir is baffled by this "riddle" but has learned to trust Frodo and so spares the intruder. Gollum comically mocks Faramir as "so wise . . . so just, so very just," but even this ridicule reminds us again of Sam likening Faramir to Gandalf.

As in other parts of Book IV, Sam's attitude to Gollum sharply contrasts Frodo's and can seem cruel. When they come with Faramir to the pool, and men of Gondor have their arrows ready, Frodo exclaims, "No! No! I beg

5. Rutledge, *Battle*, 222.

you not it," but "if Sam had dared, he would have said 'Yes,' quicker and louder." Yet as already noted there is a realism to Sam's attitude that is absolutely essential to Frodo staying alive and the ring actually being destroyed, and Sam gives us this realism again in his final words of the chapter (which come about halfway through, as in disgust he judges Gollum: "Nothing will ever be all right where that piece of misery is"). Again, this judgement might seem harsh, but it expresses a crucial, undeniable theological truth: heaven cannot be heaven if it also includes hell.

Middle-earth is neither, however, and it is one of the most important moments of the novel when Faramir solemnly declares his "doom," going on to promise that Frodo will be under his protection for at least a one-year period; moreover, whoever Frodo protects will also be protected by Faramir, as Gandalf and Aragorn had previously protected the Fellowship. Moved by this offer, Frodo pledges his own service in the solemn form of a medieval knight pledging to serve his lord, but then Faramir immediately asks the crucial question: "And now, do you take this creature, this Sméagol, under your protection?"

Frodo "bowed low" to make this promise, at which Sam "sighed" but "thoroughly approved" of the "courtesies," though "in the Shire such a matter would have required a great many more words and bows." The knowledgeable medieval narrator here (again, surely Tolkien himself) thus meets the formal requirement for Frodo to take formal stewardship of the wayward hobbit, but it is significant that as he does so, Frodo again uses the original, created hobbit's name: "I do take Sméagol under my protection." In most of the rest of this chapter he'll again be called "Gollum," but in this sacred, serious moment, Frodo is acknowledging, and pledging protection, to the hobbit which God made.

The ceremony between Faramir and Frodo, as Sam notices, has almost a ritualistic, religious quality, like the "sacramental" ceremony in the previous chapter. Perhaps this is why Faramir assents to it even while warning Frodo that Gollum is "evil." Perhaps Faramir knows the basic truth about Ilúvatar that recurs so often in *The Lord of the Rings*: it is God's very nature, part of His infinite goodness, to transform apparent evil into real good. Perhaps, finally, it is this truly religious meaning of obedient service that is demonstrated in the chapter's closing sentence, as Faramir "rose and bowed low to Frodo, and drawing the curtain passed out into the cave."

BOOK FOUR

7. JOURNEY TO THE CROSS-ROADS: "WHERE THERE'S LIFE THERE'S HOPE"

As the title of this chapter implies, it is a "journey" chapter, focused on how the three hobbits make their way south along the "other way" into Mordor. Unlike some of the novel's other journey chapters, however, this is one of the shortest chapters in the novel, as perhaps Tolkien is looking ahead to the excitement that ends Book IV. Sam does not say much on this journey, but he does deliver one of his most memorable lines in the entire novel, and the chapter closes with one of the novel's most memorable images of the triumph of good over evil.

As Faramir bids a final farewell to the hobbits, a good man but unable to give the gifts of Galadriel, Frodo again sums up the many graces Gondor has given the hobbits on their arduous journey: Faramir's friendship has turned "evil to great good."

Ithilien is again compared to Lórien when Gollum alone is to have his eyes bound but Frodo insists that all three hobbits be blindfolded.

For Sam a very important part of this good has been the resupply of food that Faramir has given, and for much of this journey we see Sam reverting to the hobbit nature long instilled by the Shire. He wants to sleep in, and awakes from dreams where he has been searching for his pipe. "Silly," he says to himself, realizing the pipe is right there in his backpack, but then the realization of his dire reality returns to him: "He had no leaf" and was "hundreds of miles from Bag End." Here again Gollum seems to serve both Frodo and Sam, exhorting them to keep moving because, "We're not in decent places."

Sam is rightly suspicious about why Gollum seems so excited to get where he wants to go, but Gollum does seem accurately aware of their present danger; as Sam asks, "Is there a storm coming? If so, it's going to be the worst there ever was." It is just after this gloomy forecast, however, that Sam delivers his great proverb: "Where there's life there's hope." Characteristically, Sam learned this from his "old Gaffer," who normally would also add, wisely, "and need of vittles." Faramir's own parting proverb—that the "Sun will soon rise above the Shadow"—seems an almost unconscious evocation of the novel's major themes.

More explicit is the chapter's conclusion, as the hobbits see, looking along the glow of a gorgeous sunset, which happens even in this desolate place, that broken statue of an old king. Servants of Mordor have cut off the head, replacing it with an old stone marked by a large red eye. Then suddenly Frodo exclaims to Sam, "Look! The King has got a crown again!" Theologians can justly compare this image to the many vain attempts in history to uncrown Christ, but Tolkien's image here directly employs nature; on the king's broken head there was now "a coronal of silver and gold," as a "plant with flowers like small white stars" now sat on the head, "as if in reverence for the fallen king." "They cannot triumph forever!" exclaims Frodo, his hope and courage renewed even as the sun sets.

8. THE STAIRS OF CIRITH UNGOL: "THE TALES THAT REALLY MATTERED"

After so few recent words from Sam, this chapter more than makes up for it! Frodo and Sam are in the fearsome rocks of "Cirith Ungol," the home of the nine wraith-riders, led out to war now by the same "haggard king whose cold hand had smitten the Ring-bearer with his deadly knife"; "the old wound throbbed with pain and a great chill spread towards Frodo's heart." As the wraith-King pauses, Frodo again feels "the command that he should put on the ring." However, in stark contrast to Book I, here there is "no longer any answer to that command in his own will," and instead Frodo touches the phial of Galadriel: "For a while, all thought of the Ring was banished from his mind."

Galadriel's gifts have clearly helped Frodo in his long battle against Sauron's will, but this chapter then reminds us that none of these gifts are more important than the friendship, and spirit, of Sam. As Frodo and Sam pause to rest "in a dark crevice" in the shadow of Cirith Ungol, this desecrated place[6] causes Frodo to express dis-enchantment in words that again, but here ironically, remind us of Tolkien's "On Fairy-Stories": "I don't like anything here at all . . . step or stone, breath or bone. Earth, air, and water all seem accursed. But so our path is laid."

It is in response to this despair that Sam gives his great discourse on "the tales that really mattered, or the ones that stay in the mind," a speech made even more famous by the fine delivery of Sean Astin in Peter Jackson's film of *The Two Towers*. Understanding Sam's speech mainly requires the simple, obvious question, "Why?"—as in why certain tales really matter, and why they stay in the heart. But more complex literary theorists would not be wrong to here hear a moment of "metafiction," fiction reflecting on the nature of fiction, and Sam does here give insight into how a reader of

---

6. My gratitude for this term to Wendell Berry's great poem, "How to Be a Poet."

BOOK FOUR

Tolkien might "apply" this story to life without falling into the trap of allegory. Here, just over midway through the hobbit's story, Sam reflects on what their journey means, again suggesting the reality of a "Meaner." This "author" is not only Tolkien, whose first age stories (on which Sam has been raised) told of great heroes such as Beren, Lúthien, and Eärendil, but also the Eternal Author who is writing the present story.

Both authors are referenced in Sam's long speech, if one knows either "Ainulindalë" or the New Testament, but first he reflects on two themes which are central to *The Lord of the Rings* and to much great literature: providence and free will. How these often-opposed notions are resolved by God is the subject of much theology, but Tolkien's thought, expressed in Sam's words, is both clear and inspiring. Unlike much theology, Sam does not oppose the two notions, instead making them both essential, but he does clarify their order. Often suggesting Tolkien's conception of God as "the Great Writer of the Story," Fleming Rutledge replies to Frodo's key question—"Is the story already written?"—with this insightful passage:

> There is truly a sense in which "the story is already written." . . . The ever-present sense of an overarching purpose pulling all the threads together is a theme that pervades the book. "In *everything* God works for good with those . . . who are called according to his purpose," as St. Paul wrote (Rom 8:28).[7]

Yet Sam himself is certainly no systematic theologian. In his youth, perhaps remembering the "there and back" adventure that was *The Hobbit*, Sam had thought of exciting tales "as a kind of sport" that "wonderful folk . . . went out and looked for." But now he knows this is not the way of tales "that really mattered," for as Frodo has said, their "paths were laid out that way," and many challenges they face are given, not chosen. Courageous choice was still essential, though, because characters in such stories "had lots of chances . . . of turning back, only they didn't." "Like us," Sam here interjects, concluding by wondering "what sort of tale we've fallen into?"

Frodo's reply again stresses courage, for no one wants to know whether a tale is "happy-ending or sad-ending" while reading it, nor would one want the characters "inside a story" to know either. "No, sir, of course not," agrees Sam, citing the courage of both Beren and Eärendil against great obstacles. This leads Sam to the key insight that inside the phial from Galadriel is some of the same light that enlightened these past heroes, and to

---

7. Rutledge, *Battle*, 232.

realize that the theological narrative that Tolkien began with Ilúvatar goes on still: "Why, to think of it, we're in the same story now!" Bernthal has the universal application: "Everything that has happened since the beginning of the world is part of a story that tells Christians who they are."[8]

Frodo cautions that the part of each player in even the greatest of tales ends, but then Sam imagines a child reading "by the fireside" and saying, "Let's hear about Frodo and the Ring!" Far from being puffed up with pride or fame, Frodo is genuinely humbled, and laughs the laugh of "consolation" that Tolkien's fairy stories intend: "A long clear laugh right from the heart." "Such a sound had not been heard in those places since Sauron came to Middle-earth," the narrator comments, accentuating the theological theme by adding that "to Sam suddenly it seemed as if all the stones were listening." Frodo simply continues the consolation by imagining what many readers must say of Sam: "I want to hear more about Sam, dad. Why didn't they put in more of his talk, dad? That's what I like, it makes me laugh. And Frodo wouldn't have got far without Sam, would he dad?"

Sam is similarly humbled, but Frodo stresses the seriousness of his comical comments, and the two friends are back in the present tale when Frodo reminds them that they "are still stuck in the worst places of the story." Some readers might here give up, while others, on a least their second time through the story, might console themselves by counting Frodo and Sam amongst the heroes of legend who have a "happy ending." Whether one counts the "brave ring-bearer" or the "stout-hearted" Sam as the "true hero" of the story, we can be consoled by their ending. Yet it is Sam who complicates matters here by for once speaking kindly of Gollum, acknowledging that he "might be good in a tale," and even wondering "if he thinks he's the hero or the villain." For once speaking charitably to Gollum, Sam cries into the darkness: "Gollum! Would you like to be the hero—now where's he got to again?"

Sam's cry is not silliness or vain hope. On the contrary, as Wood explains well:

> Sam has here plumbed the depth of real hope. The "great tales" stand apart from mere adventures because they belong to the One Great Story. It is a story not only of those who fight heroically against evil, but also of those who are unwilling to exterminate

---

8. Bernthal, *Sacramental*, 171.

such an enemy as Gollum. As Sam discerns, this Tale finds a surprising place even for evil.[9]

Second-time readers know Gollum is away likely plotting the villainy of the next two chapters, but they also know that Gollum is the hobbit who, at least in a physical sense, will complete the most heroic action of this story: the destruction of the ring. Both facts must be kept in mind to appreciate why Tolkien, in his letters, describes Sam's subsequent treatment of Gollum in this chapter as "the most tragic moment in the Tale."[10]

If we do gain this understanding, we might further see why, in this chapter, after Gollum returns and sees Sam and Frodo sleeping together peacefully, Tolkien's narrator describes Gollum as "an old weary hobbit, shrunken by the years that had carried him far beyond his time, beyond friends and kin, and the fields and streams of youth, an old starved pitiable thing." Readers feel pity for Gollum as Bilbo did in the dark cave at their first meeting, pity not typically given to villains of a tale. Even without the "caress" of Frodo's knee by which Sméagol shows real affection for his master, it is pity for the eventually manifest faults of all three hobbits that we must feel when Sam awakes to what he interprets as "pawing at master." Gollum, he accuses, has been "sneaking off and sneaking back," and his identity as an "old villain" no longer seems in doubt.

Again, the truth of that label in the next two chapters, and Sam's own heroism, makes it easy to simply accept this judgement. Yet surely there is also wisdom in Frodo's counsel as Gollum starts to call himself a "sneak." Frodo cautions, "Don't take names to yourself, Sméagol. . . . It's unwise, whether true or false." Why so? Perhaps, and here again theologians can do much with the traditional image of the "stairs" of purgatory, our ultimate identity can only be determined by God. Ilúvatar's light is in the darkest places, and we must reach for it to find the courage to go on. The application of the images in *The Lord of the Rings*, and insights offered by its character and themes, are part of the consolation offered by God's eucatastrophe.

9. SHELOB'S LAIR: "THE LADY'S GIFT!"

Ironically, despite Tolkien's apparent regret of Sam's suspicion and mistrust, it is the very next chapter where Gollum proves his treachery. For very

---

9. Wood, *Gospel*, 148.
10. Tolkien, *Letters*, 465.

consciously he brings Frodo to "a tunnel" that he insists is the "only way" into Mordor. But he "did not speak its name: Torech Ungol, Shelob's Lair." Inside the dark tunnel, even Frodo's call to "Sméagol . . . fell dead almost as it left its lips." Any doubt of Gollum's dominant nature, his real intentions, are eliminated by his violent malice at chapter's end. As the fearsome spider, Shelob, is about to attack Frodo, Gollum attacks Sam "from behind," the "old game" that usually allowed him to murder his victim. This time, though, Sam breaks free, because Gollum makes the mistake of "speaking and gloating," not being able to resist repeating Sam's name for him in the previous chapter. Spite ripping from Gollum's mouth before he actually spits on Sam and turns one of his own "names" upon the less friendly hobbit, Gollum shrieks: "He's got you, you nasty filthy little sneak!"

If the treachery of Gollum is thus made clear, the pure evil of absolute darkness shrouds the creature to whom he has brought the "fresh, sweet meat" of the hobbits. "Shelob the Great" "agelong had dwelt" in this tunnel, the "last child of Ungoliant to trouble the unhappy world," a reference to the ancient spider who attacked the two trees of light in Valinor early in *The Silmarillion*. Interpreted literally, that would make Shelob very old, but Tolkien for once is not historically precise. The more important point is that "she served none but herself, drinking the blood of Elves and men." As readers learn from Treebeard in Book III, there are many powers of good and evil not on the side of Gandalf or Sauron in the present conflict. Sauron does know about her, but is happy to let her alone as a natural guard on the border of Mordor, one far more vicious than any that even he could devise. The malevolent will of Shelob is often stressed, as Frodo and Sam feel her desire to consume them as soon as they are in the tunnel.

When Shelob attacks, it is another ancient power, the phial that Galadriel gave to Frodo, that now comes to light. Sam reminds Frodo that is it there in his pocket, and Frodo recalls Galadriel's promise that it will be, "*A light when all other lights go out!*" When the phial comes to light, it is truly spectacular:

> It began to burn, and kindled to a silver flame, a minute heart of dazzling light, as though Eärendil had himself come down from the high sunset paths with the last Silmaril upon his brow. The darkness receded from it until it seemed to shine in the center of a globe of airy crystal, and the hand that held it sparkled with white fire.

In this extraordinary moment, ancient Elvish voices also speak through Frodo: "*Aiya Eärendil elenion ancalima!*" Tolkien stresses that these are not Frodo's own words, by adding that Frodo "knew not what he had spoken; for it seemed that another voice spoke through his, clear, untroubled by the foul air of the pit." This same point is also made, in the next chapter, when Sam utters a similar cry and Tolkien's narrator, in the passive voice, comments that "then his tongue was loosed and his voice cried out in a language which he did not know." Only after five lines of Elvish does he stagger to his feet and "was Samwise the hobbit, Hamfast's son, again."

Such moments are important reminders of the providential "good powers" still forceful in Middle-earth, but Sam's own free choices are also highlighted in the chapter, again through error. It's easy to miss, amidst all the tension, but just after slashing through Shelob's cobwebs with Sting and running to flee the tunnel, Frodo commands Sam to "be the guard," to hold up the phial "and watch." Sam fails not through conscious disobedience, but when he returns "to his long habit of secrecy" and puts the phial back in his pocket. The instant he hides the light, Shelob attacks Frodo again, and when Sam rushes to his Master's defense, then Gollum grabs him "from behind." What good comes from the evil of this error?

This is not an easy question to answer. Its challenge is at the heart of the "choices" that Sam must make in the next chapter. But by this point in the novel, we have the example of Gandalf's fall with the Balrog, which seems so horrible at the time, but we have also seen the return of the even stronger spiritually Gandalf the White. We also have the example of Aragorn's choice to follow Merry and Pippen, rather than Frodo and Sam; after the evil of Boromir's murder, there is so much good that yet comes out of Book III.

Here, near the end of Book IV, the spectacular light of Galadriel's phial, which Shelob cannot tolerate, reminds us of the natural power of light to dispel darkness, and the pain caused by Shelob's and Gollum's assault awakens and helps us see the exceptional courage and goodness inside Sam, goodness sometimes obscured outwardly by his humility. We see the full virtue of his character in the next chapter. Here one might apply scripture from the beloved apostle who gives the Bible's most famous discourse on light: "Every one that doeth evil hateth the light . . . but he that doeth truth cometh to the light, that his deeds may be made manifest, that they are wrought in God" (John 3:20–21).

10. THE CHOICES OF MASTER SAMWISE: "MAY I BE FORGIVEN!"

The suspenseful choice anticipated at the end of chapter 9, combined with the title of this chapter, causes us to expect this final chapter in Book IV to be a portrayal of Sam's climactic choices. Largely the chapter fulfills this hope, for it might be the novel's closest focus upon Sam's character, while Jackson's terrible decision to move it into his third film diminished this focus. Structurally, the chapter's themes make sense as the completion of Frodo's wondering which way to go at the start of chapter 1 in Book VI, or even Aragorn struggling to decide, in chapter 10 of Book III whether to try to rescue Pippen and Merry from the orcs or follow the ringbearer (another irrational choice eventually revealed as a great good).

Yet this chapter opens with an action that seems no choice at all. Sam, seeing Shelob attacking Frodo, "did not wait to wonder what was to be done," but simply charges after Shelob with great courage in complete disregard of his life. Sam charges, "reeling like a drunken man," hardly an image of conscientious choice. Tolkien also likens Sam to "some desperate small creature," and possible reference to Bilbo becomes explicit when we are told that "Shelob was not as dragons are," with no soft spot to penetrate. Rather than the heroic marksmanship of Bard, here "She" herself lowers herself on Sting, so it is Her will rather than Sam's that makes the critical "choice."

Yet if Tolkien is never simplistic, nor does he ever let us forget (a point we must return to with Gollum on Mount Doom) that present choices are often, in an important sense, *caused* by previous choices, which prepare our wills to act what is most necessary. Sam's desperate courage is a good example, but several other examples are highlighted in this moment of truth. Sam again thinks of the phial of Galadriel, and recalls hearing the crying of the Elves "under the stars in the beloved shadows of the Shire, and the music of Elves" at Rivendell. Even Sam's reverence for the gifts of Galadriel is a choice, in a sense, though here we again note that it is "some remote voice" that now speaks through him, as his "tongue was loosed and his voice cried in a language which he did not know."

Tolkien's narrator again suggests the "transcendent dimension" that Sam has given us before, and this chapter particularly shows Sam enacting, rather than explaining, Tolkien's profound, deeply Augustinian understanding of the connection God creates between free will and predestination. Later in the chapter, as Sam makes the difficult choice to carry the ring forward after Frodo's apparent death, he himself is becoming a hero like those

BOOK FOUR

in the great tales that he spoke about in "The Stairs of Cirith Ungol." "They didn't choose themselves," Sam here stresses, reminding us of the Augustinian notion of "prevenient grace" that prepare the choices that, within God's providential plan, the will should make. Tolkien's primary tongue is not theology, though, but Elvish language poetry. So here Sam cries out for the protection of the Valar, "Elbereth," to whom Galadriel is devoted, and she seems to objectively protect Sam against Shelob. Yet as earlier with Frodo, it is Sam's "indomitable spirit" that "set [the phial] its potency in motion," so that its light "flamed like a star" and sends Shelob scurrying away.

Choice and gift, valid synonyms for free will and providence, thus remain very much mixed in Sam's defeat of Shelob. After Frodo is found bound, unconscious, and apparently dead, the choice facing Sam seems very stark. As he puts it, "What shall I do, what shall I do?" To answer this question, Sam recalls his own words at the end of Book I, when Frodo was departing without him: "I have something to do before the end. I must see it through, sir, if you understand." The essence of Sam's mission has always been to stay with his master, but here he is convinced by facial appearance that Frodo is dead. Sam's decision here to go on alone, to continue trying to destroy the ring, is not based on pride, fear, or any lack of courage; rather, relentless logic drives Sam on: "It's sit here till they come and kill me over master's body, and gets It; or take It and go.... Then take It, it is!"

Sam does put on the ring, and it is fascinating to compare how it affects him compared to the other hobbit ringbearers, Bilbo and Frodo, or even to Tom Bombadil, especially when Sam later freely gives up the ring. Even immediately, there are key differences: Sam does not remain visible, like Tom Bombadil, but nor is he visible to the servants of Sauron, as Frodo was on Weathertop. Sam's "hearing was sharpened while sight was dimmed," and "he knew that somewhere an Eye was searching for him." The key point, here, though, is something we haven't heard before. Overhearing some orcs, Sam understands their language, and the narrator comments:

> Perhaps the Ring gave understanding of tongues, or simply understanding, especially of the servants of Sauron its maker, so that if he gave heed, he understood and translated the thought to himself. Certainly the Ring had grown greatly in power as it approached the places of its forging; but one thing it did not confer, and that was courage.

Sam does show courage in going on without Frodo, but we should note here that he also makes just one wish to Galadriel: "If only I could have my wish, my one wish, to go back and find him." There is also a fascinating reference to the mirror of Galadriel, as suddenly he saw that he was in the picture that was revealed to him in the mirror of Galadriel in Lórien: "Frodo with a pale face lying fast asleep under a great dark cliff." Or "fast asleep he had thought then," but now Sam is sure that Frodo is actually dead!

Even before we learn that Sam's judgement here is in error, we should recall what Frodo learned from the elf Gildor when Sam first met the Elves: "Go not to the Elves for counsel." On her own mirror, the elf-queen Galadriel had said that "it shows things that were, and things that are, and things that yet may be. But which it is that he sees, even the wisest cannot always tell." Frodo's present reality does become dramatically clear here, however, when one Orc tells the other, "This fellow isn't dead," noting that Shelob binds with cords in order to eat live meat: "She doesn't eat dead meat, nor such cold blood." The self-rebuke of "half-wise" Sam is quick and insightful: "You fool, he isn't dead, and your heart knew it. Don't trust your head, Samwise, it is not the best part of you." Even readers without any knowledge of St. Augustine on the soul can understand that Sam's intellect failed him, but the consistent choices of his will (a word often synonymous with "heart" in English literature) has returned him to the right course of action. Sam's return comes through mysterious help from Galadriel, whom he calls upon directly before using the phial of light that she gave to Frodo.

As Book IV closes, Frodo remains bound, captured by the orcs, and readers are in suspenseful uncertainty as to his fate. This obvious example of dramatic structure, since we won't learn Frodo's fate until reading all of Book V, was somehow missed by Peter Jackson, whose films present these final two chapters in his third rather than second film, but readers with Tolkien's heart for Sam should not be in doubt. The gifts of Galadriel are real, and her light has given light even in the darkest of places. We don't know yet how wearing the ring will affect Sam; as Fleming Rutledge puts it: "Thus the complexity of the novel grows; we know what the Ring has been doing to the highly educated but trained Frodo. What will it now do to the simple gardener?"[11] Jackson avoids such complexity, and potential audience confusion, via a similar strategy as the omission of Bombadil; his Samwise simply never puts on the ring. As readers we can contrast the effects of the ring on Bilbo, Tom, Frodo, and Sam. Perhaps more important than such understanding, however, is our sure knowledge that Sam has put

---

11. Rutledge, *Battle*, 238.

BOOK FOUR

on the ring only because he loves his master, Frodo, as much as God, and his Gaffer, love him.

INTERLUDE

Tolkien's division of the plot, with Gandalf, Aragorn, et al on one front and Frodo, Sam, and Gollum on another, is by this point in the novel familiar. The many extraordinary events of Book V, in a way, remind us of the miraculous consolations possible to the bleak conclusion of Book IV. Yet the problem remains, which we noted between Books II and IV—of how the second plot can possibly be as engaging, yet alone as exciting, as the plot with far more characters. After Book V, this problem seems even greater, because Merry and Pippen do such extraordinary things, as does Éowyn disguised as "Dernhelm." How can Sam possibly match them? In Book VI, Tolkien develops the question of who is the true hero of this novel, a question which in many ways pivots on Sam's relationship to Frodo and Gollum.

At the start of Book VI, there is a key passage that connects the two plots. As Sam looks West, thinking of the original fellowship, the narrator comments:

> Out westward in the world it was drawing to noon upon the fourteenth day of March in the Shire-reckoning. And even now Aragorn was leading the black fleet from Pelargir, and Merry was riding with the Rohirrim down the Stonewain Valley, while in Minas Tirith flames were rising and Pippin watched the madness growing in the eyes of Denethor. Yet amid all their cares and fear the thoughts of their friends turned constantly to Frodo and Sam. They were not forgotten. But they were far beyond aid, and no thought could yet bring any help to Samwise Hamfast's son; he was utterly alone.

The passage allows at least three key insights. First, that the events of Books V and VI are happening at the same time. Second, that Tolkien is carefully dating these events, up to the destruction of the Ring on the universal day of "eucatastrophe" that is March 25; this passage is the only place where calendar date is given before the appendices, and March 25 could have its own resonance as "Laetare Sunday," if falling on the Lenten Sunday that looks forward with hope to Easter, though in the pre-Vatican II Catholic calendar it is a feast day for martyrs. Sam often seems likely to be counted among such martyrs as he and Frodo approach Mount Doom, and their journey will give many opportunities for profound reflection on hope. Finally, the passage also reminds us that the Fellowship is not broken, that "their friends" often think of Frodo and Sam, just as the communion of saints truly care for each other. Yet at the start of Book VI, Sam feels "utterly alone," as even saints often do in this world.

Such applications are consoling and no doubt intended by our "Author," but for us, in this world, to remain a "friend to the novel," like the reader of Tolkien's letters noted in my preface, we must be with Sam in his moments of despair in order to recover the extraordinary consolation that Book VI offers.

Book Six

1. THE TOWER OF CIRITH UNGOL: "ABOVE ALL SHADOWS RIDES THE SUN"

This chapter opens with Tolkien reminding us both that we have been in this place before, as we pick up almost where Book VI left off, and also that things have changed. The title is the first indication of this dual purpose, as for the first time in the novel words from an earlier chapter title are used again, but also that have moved beyond the multiple "two towers" to "the tower," the final construction that must be passed before Mount Doom; "beyond all towers" will be the key phrase in the great song that Sam sings in the great song at the heart of the chapter.

Sam is still outside the locked gates where the orcs are holding Frodo, but "then he had been on fire, desperate and furious; now he was shivering and cold." He "no longer had any doubt about his duty" to save Frodo or die trying, but in this "land of darkness" his "fear of the orcs . . . returned." Central in this chapter will be Sam's attitude to the Ring, which normally some fear prompts putting on, but here Sam first puts it on "without any clear purpose." Soon he takes it off, if only in his own mind "to see more clearly," but it is one constant thought, which we have seen so many times in the novel, that again guides Sam's will: "His love for Frodo rose above all other thoughts." This love begins in his nature, but is perfected by divine grace. As Ralph Wood stresses, Sam above all other characters in the novel shows how the four practical virtues are completed by the three theological virtues.[1]

Sam does begin to be tempted by the Ring in ways similar to the other heroes of the novel. It gnaws "at his will and reason," and he even starts to imagine himself as "Samwise the Strong, Hero of the Age." But in such

---

1. Wood, *Gospel*, 117–55.

Recovering Consolation

moments, which again remind us of how the ring tempted Gandalf and Galadriel, again "it was the love of his master that helped most to hold him firm." We have previously noticed his exceptional hobbit humility, but Tolkien (who himself loved gardening) stresses how the simple, commonplace life that Sam led in the Shire had prepared him for this moment of trial: "One small garden of a free gardener was all his need and due, not a garden swollen to a realm; his own hands to use, not the hands of others to command." Sam knows who he is, though he plays with the identity that the stupid orcs give him after they argue amongst themselves and try to hide from the supposedly fearsome Sam: as with Shelob, he here will boldly act, at one point calling to the orc leader: "Tell Captain Shagrat that the great Elf-Warrior has called, with his elf-sword too!"

Sam's courage leads him up the tower where Frodo is being held, but it seems "a dead end" when doors there are locked. In despair, "to his own surprise," Sam starts to sing. What moves his heart to do so "he could not tell," but this is not quite the same as the previous moments in the novel when an objective voice speaks through him. For it is "words of his own" that come out as his voice changes from a "forlorn and weary hobbit" into something like "the clear song of an Elven-Lord." Unlike many previous poems and songs in which Sam or others are commenting on others' stories, here the poem is clearly spoken from inside the "one story" that Sam had realized they are in back on "the stairs of Cirith Ungol." The first eight-line stanza evokes the universal symbols of Tolkien's legendarium:

> In western lands beneath the Sun
> the flowers may rise in Spring,
> the trees may bud, the waters run,
> the merry finches sing.
> Or there maybe 'tis cloudless night
> and swaying beeches bear
> the Elven-stars as jewels white
> amid their branching hair.

The second, concluding section relates more specifically to Sam's present place, and puts into poetry the great prose passage that the novel's next chapter will make so famous:

> Though here at journey's end I lie
> in darkness buried deep,
> beyond all towers strong and high,
> beyond all mountains steep,

above all shadows rides the Sun
and Stars for ever dwell:
I will not say the Day is done,
nor bid the Stars farewell.

As Sam starts to sing the second stanza again, he "thought that he had heard a faint voice answering him." After battling more orcs, he'll eventually learn that this was the voice of the semi-conscious Frodo. The friends' reunion, however, seems at first marred by the Ring. For as soon as Frodo learns that Sam has it, that the orcs have not taken everything from him, he reverts to words that remind us of Bilbo struggling to give the ring back to Gandalf, or even of Gollum trying to regain his "precious" possession: "Give it to me! . . . Give it to me at once! You can't have it!" For the first and only time in the history of the Ring, it is given up freely, and it is solely out of concern for his master's burdens that Sam adds, "If it's too hard a job, I could share it with you." "No you won't you thief," cries Frodo, before apologizing and recognizing that his harsh response has been caused by "the horrible power of the ring."

Frodo again wishes the Ring had never been found, but by chapter's end we again see how this evil has been turned to good through the extraordinary friendship forged between Sam and Frodo. They turn the now familiar name of "Elbereth" to a password for the trapdoor inside where Sam finds Frodo, then both speak Elvish lines that, with the phial of Galadriel, break the will of the "Watchers"—three-headed stone monsters who, like the Trinitarian parody at the bottom of Dante's Hell—guard any exit from Hell. Readers can recognize that Sam and Frodo are now free not because of material magic, but rather in the consolation of Elvish love.

2. THE LAND OF SHADOW: "ALL WE WANT IS LIGHT AND WATER"

Rather than exiting hell, as Dante does in fleeing his three-headed parody of the Trinity, Frodo and Sam must hide from Nazgûl and searching Orcs as they enter Mordor itself. This is the "land of shadow," that they have dreaded ever since chapter 2 of the novel, when they first learned that "the shadow of the past" would haunt their present. Yet unlike the purpose of repetition in chapter 1 of Book VI, here Tolkien returns to his more common practice of seeming to announce an obvious topic, but then using the chapter itself to develop another meaning. Mordor is a land of desolate evil, of course, but we are constantly surprised when this land also retains signs of life. As with Gollum, evil cannot completely obliterate created good. Aspects of this land, as with all creation, are recovered in a consolation which prepares us for the great eucatastrophe to come in the next chapter. As elsewhere in the novel, Sam plays a central role in this recovery, though certainly he grows in understanding that he is not alone.

The first obvious sign of the focus upon this theme here comes when Frodo and Sam follow Bilbo in taking another "leap in the dark," as they leap under a bridge, unsure of what lies below, in order to avoid the orcs rushing out to recapture them. Sam "would have laughed, if he had dared," but both he and Frodo are surprised that they have landed "into the last thing that they had expected: a tangle of thorny bushes." Theological allegory here seems almost inevitable, as our martyrs gain a "crown of thorns." Yet one of the broad points of my book, that allegorical meanings cannot supersede the recovered concrete because Tolkien would never attempt to imagine his work as a "secular scripture," is here driven home (to wit) when Sam comments that he "didn't know as anything grew in Mordor," but these thorns are a "foot long." Sam wishes he still had the orc mail shirt (a shirt we will hear of again in this chapter) that he and Frodo has discarded to lighten their load as they escaped. Frodo does point to a "spiritual sense" here by noting that not even thick leather can keep out these thorns, but the sharper point (to pun again) is surely the painful puncture of these real thorns. Yet they are certainly examples of apparent evil doing surprising good, for these thorns do allow Frodo and Sam to escape recapture and be relatively uninjured after their fall.

Other natural gifts are also found in Mordor, but with them are still Sting and the phial of Galadriel, and the gifts of "the Lady" become especially important. The first example of this comes when Sam gives the cold Frodo the cloak from his back, noting that the cloak's high quality comes because "it was made by the Lady." Again, Catholic theological interpreters, from Fr. Murray on, cannot help seeing in Sam's love of the Lady the popular Catholic devotion to Mary. Nor are theological interpreters wrong to relate the irrevocable goodness in even the land of Mordor to God's choice to redeem all of nature in Mary's Immaculate Conception, as Tolkien will highlight by making so specific the date of March 25, the Feast of the Annunciation.

Yet within this chapter of the novel, much simpler natural goods are recovered: light and water. Again, Sam makes this point very clear by saying,

Book Six

"If only the Lady could see us or hear us, I'd say to her: 'Your Ladyship, all we want is light and water: just clean water and plain daylight, better than any jewels, begging your pardon.'" As the chapter develops, both gifts are found, even here in Mordor, and Sam has no doubt as to why: "If ever I see the Lady again, I will tell her!" Yet readers have no way of knowing whether Sam is correct to think that Galadriel watches over him, or whether nature in Mordor simply reflects the creative power of the Creator. Again, an allegorical comparison to Mary is simply beyond Tolkien's novel; not that Catholics cannot think of it, but especially for them Galadriel's inferiority to Mary should be obvious. Mary's central role in nature, always connected to her role as the Mother of God, can be known for certain, dogmatically, unlike the complex story and intention of Galadriel.[2]

What we *can* know for certain in the novel is the goodness of the recovered light and water, and the real hope still possible. Sam has often had to be optimistic as Frodo's burdens make him pessimistic, often seeing especially this last part of the journey as especially hopeless. Sam does have to be realistic, telling Frodo here of Gollum's treachery with Shelob after the "black sneak" (as one of the orcs searching for the escaped hobbits calls him) is seen again. This orc kills his "companion," whose own attempt to shoot Gollum seems to have been thwarted, ironically, by the orc-shirt that Sam had dropped. Sam can't be happy about this, and it is with wry honesty that he comments, after the orc's death, "If this nice friendliness would spread about in Mordor, half our trouble would be over." Yet given the oft noted good of Gollum remaining alive, shortly to become obvious at Mount Doom, Tolkien's main point here seems again to be the recurrent theme of evil doing good, even against its will. Good is active even as we personally face great evil, as Tolkien's narrator stresses amidst Sam and Frodo's ideal by also telling us, "The Lord of the Ringwraiths had met his doom." Sam and Frodo would never guess that this extraordinary feat was achieved by so unlikely a pair as Éowyn and Merry, but the orcs' conversation has referenced "bad" news from the war; Sam exults, "He's not having it all his own way. His darkness is breaking up out in the world out there."

Possibly Sam's greatest and certainly most oft-quoted affirmation of hope comes later in this chapter, as Frodo goes to sleep under rocks; There Sam

---

2. This dogmatic certainty inspires rather than curtails creativity; for an example, see Gerard Manley Hopkins great poem on Mary, "May Magnificat."

sat silent till deep night fell. Then at last, to keep himself awake, he crawled from the hiding-place and looked out. The land seemed full of creaking and cracking and sly noises, but there was no sound of voice or of foot. Far above the Ephel Dúath in the West the night-sky was still dim and pale. There, peeping among the cloud-wrack above a dark tower high up in the mountains, Sam saw a white star twinkle for a while. The beauty of it smote his heart, as he looked up out of the forsaken land, and hope returned to him. For like a shaft, clear and cold, the thought pierced him that in the end the Shadow was only a small and passing thing: there was light and high beauty for ever beyond its reach.

This passage offers transcendent, infinite meaning. In terms of symbolic reference to the sovereignty of God, perhaps this moment makes the second chapter of Book VI as important, thematically, as the second chapters of Books I and II. Ralph Wood's comment on this key moment is insightful:

> Sam is not bound by the logic of the obvious. He sees that star and shadow are not locked in a dualistic combat of equals, nor are they engaged in a battle whose outcome remains uncertain. He discerns the deep and paradoxical truth that the dark has no meaning apart from the light. Light is both the primal and the final reality, not the night that seeks to quench it. The single flickering star, Sam sees, penetrates and defines the gargantuan gloom. "The Light shines in the darkness, and the darkness has not overcome it (John 1:5).[3]

Here, in the complete silence and darkness of Mordor, Sam knows in his heart, supported by sight of the stars in the sky, that God's goodness is stronger than any evil, and remains true and beautiful beyond any storms or shadows. The theme here seems the same as in Sam's song of the previous chapter, but now expressed in the narrator's prose rather than Sam's poetry. Romantics might value the poetry more, but Tolkien's narrator seems to assert the opposite, continuing the passage just quoted by adding, "His song in the Tower had been defiance rather than hope; for then he was thinking of himself." The point might again be Catholic aesthetics, as the universal is valued above the personal. Yet Tolkien also makes this moment intensely personal when at the end of this passage Sam put "away all fear," and "cast himself into a deep untroubled sleep." He and Frodo "woke together, hand in hand." Rarely has literary art ever made more concrete, more real, than

---

3. Wood, *Gospel*, 145.

the seemingly ludicrous claim of John the apostle: "Perfect love casteth out all fear" (1 John 4:18).

This theological high point in the journey is reinforced, as the chapter closes, with several other plot details. In addition to the stars the hobbits do see Mount Doom in the distance, and behind it "a vast shadow, ominous as a thunder-cloud," the dungeons of Sauron. Yet even "shadow" itself, as a concrete reality rather than theological symbol, is redeemed when Sam and Frodo hide from the searching orcs, and there find water, "under the shadow" of a cliff. Ultimate humiliation seems to come when Sam and Frodo have to march with orcs going to war, but this evil turns to good when the orc-convoy turns to confusion and the hobbits can hide, then escape. Even darkness itself aids their escape, and in a final moving image Frodo then falls asleep in "a shallow pit." Even nature normally constructed as a grave becomes a good here, by becoming not a place of death but instead life-giving rest. Consolation is recovered prior to the hobbits' final test.

3. MOUNT DOOM: "NO WORDS"

The concluding "shallow pit" image could easily be interpreted, though it would be a misinterpretation, as foreshadowing the impending conclusion of Frodo's life, journey, and the novel itself. This famous chapter's title could also similarly be misinterpreted, if "doom" is understood in the popular sense of ending, as seemingly in the previous chapter when we are told the Nazgûl king "met his doom." Book VI is filled with further "false endings," in which the novel's characters believe the end is near but their Author, whether Tolkien or Ilúvatar, has other plans.

Historically, the word "doom" mainly derived from "doomsday," the final day in which God judges all. All the complexities of time and eternity were thus evoked, and the providence of God is foregrounded, as when the final scene of *King Lear* compares its action to an "image of that horror" that is Doomsday.[4] In the same play, Lear famously feels himself "bound upon a wheel of fire,"[5] a commonplace image that Tolkien seems to use when Frodo begins to see the ring "in my mind all the time, like a wheel of fire." Modern critics often take this as the "wheel of fortune," but the medieval commonplace, which Tolkien likely knew, is the "wheel of providence" described by Boethius's *Consolation of Philosophy*. The point here

4. Shakespeare, *King Lear*, 5.3.238.
5. Shakespeare, *King Lear*, 4.6.40.

Recovering Consolation

is not simply linguistic. As *The Lord of the Rings* so often shows, God uses temporary evil to bring about lasting good. Two themes that can be traced directly back to the "Ainulindalë" stand out in this chapter: first, the surprising nature of hobbits, and finally the sovereignty of God.

The first point will be seen in all three of the main hobbits in this story, and we will again reflect on which is the "hero," which the "villain" of the story, for it is surely a surprise that this dark, climactic chapter begins with Sam musing on the Elves again. The entire first sentence of the chapter is worth quoting:

> Sam put his ragged orc-cloak under his master's head, and covered them both with the grey robe of Lórien; and as he did so his thoughts went out to that fair land, and to the Elves, and he hoped that the cloth woven by their hands might have some virtue to keep them hidden beyond all hope in this wilderness of fear.

The key phrase here is "beyond all hope" for, particularly after the magnificent song and universal prose to hope, it is somewhat surprising that even Sam here loses hope. Tolkien's narrator comments, "Never for long had hope died in his staunch heart, and always until now he had taken some thought for their return." Now, however, even Sam thinks "there could be no return," for the hobbits are simply out of supplies, if they do make it to Mount Doom, and Sam in this chapter throws out his beloved cooking gear. Yet "even as hope died in Sam, or seemed to die, it was turned to a new strength." Sam's "will hardened," and in perhaps the most memorable evidence of this he carries Frodo on his back up Mount Doom. Bernthal compares Sam here to Simon of Cyrene, carrying Christ's cross, an application which seems valid even though Frodo is about to prove that he is not an allegorical "Christ-figure."[6]

In this crucial moment, the unity of Sam's enthusiasm and God's will, given to him, produces one of the novel's most memorable passages:

> As Frodo clung upon his back, arms loosely about his neck, legs clasped firmly under his arms, Sam staggered to his feet; and then to his amazement he felt the burden light. He had feared that he would have barely strength to lift his master alone, and beyond that he had expected to share in the dreadful dragging weight of the accursed Ring. But it was not so. Whether because Frodo was so worn by his long pains, wound of knife, and venomous sting, and sorrow, fear, and homeless wandering, or because some gift

---

6. Bernthal, *Sacramental*, 259.

of final strength was given to him, Sam lifted Frodo with no more difficulty than if he were carrying a hobbit-child pig-a-back in some romp on the lawns or hayfields of the Shire. He took a deep breath and started off.

Biblically alert readers hear Jesus's paradoxical promise, "My yoke is easy, and my burden light" (Matt 11:30). Rutledge again sees "the unseen Providential power at work even in the very heart of the domain of the Evil One."[7] On this "last stage of their journey," Sam and Frodo are both "in pain" like all martyrs, and we expect their impending death, but God clearly provides consolation. Frodo and Sam experience "something akin to the Christian mystery of finding their power in their utter darkness."[8]

Surprisingly, neither dies, but this is just one of many surprises that Tolkien here gives us. Frodo's claim of the ring, refusing to destroy it and thus definitively refuting any notion that he is an allegory of Christ, is the best-known surprise of the chapter, but some also more directly concern Sam. The most important of these, however, is less well known today, mainly because Peter Jackson omitted it from his film. Understandably wanting to condense the action, Jackson's film simply shows Gollum knocking out Sam and then biting the ring off of Frodo's hand before falling to his doom. Tolkien's novel, however, first shows Sam fighting Gollum down and the poor creature pleading for his life. Sam had often desired Gollum's death, and even in this chapter it is simply common sense when Sam does not throw away his sword for fear that Gollum will find it, but this is the first time when it would be relatively simple to actually kill Gollum. Surprisingly, Sam does not, and Tolkien gives us this crucial explanation:

> Sam's hand wavered. His mind was hot with wrath and the memory of evil. It would be just to slay this treacherous, murderous creature, just and many times deserved; and also it seemed the only safe thing to do. But deep in his heart there was something that restrained him: he could not strike this thing lying in the dust, forlorn, ruinous, utterly wretched. He himself, though only for a little while, had borne the Ring, and now dimly he guessed the agony of Gollum's shriveled mind and body, enslaved to that Ring, unable to find peace or relief ever in life again. But Sam had no words to express what he felt.

---

7. Rutledge, *Battle*, 333.
8. Wood, *Gospel*, 111.

Recovering Consolation

As this passage makes clear, the point of this surprising scene is not simply a change in Sam; rather, it is the parallel pity for Gollum that comes to each of the three hobbit ringbearers, Bilbo, Frodo and now Sam. In a very direct way, Sam's choice here is obviously essential to Gollum being alive in a few moments to actually destroy the ring. At the end of the chapter, Frodo acknowledges, "But for him, Sam, I could not have destroyed the ring," and for the third time in the novel he quotes Gandalf that "Gollum may have something yet to do." Readers fully understand, by this point, that Gandalf has seen a providential plan "laid out" (as Sam and Frodo put it in their discourse on stories) ever since the surprising finding of the ring by Bilbo, and his crucial "leap in the dark" when *he* could easily have killed Gollum. Pity, the virtue being sanctified in each of the hobbits, is clearly crucial to this providential plan, as Gandalf has long stressed. So Sam's pity in this scene is not sentimental emotion, but virtuous mercy that makes a major difference in the history of Middle-earth.

The sovereignty of God is also suggested in Tolkien's novel by how Gollum falls into the fires of Mount Doom. He is clearly not pushed by Frodo, nor can we say simply that he "lost his balance." Rather, he falls "as his eyes were lifted up to gloat on his prize," a fairly clear instance of the biblical commonplace, "pride comes before the fall" (Prov 16:18). Because pride is the major vice opposed to pity (and humility, the other key hobbit virtue being "sanctified"), we don't have to posit God's direct providential action in Gollum's fall; it is simply the reward of sin, an action linked to every choice that Gollum has made since murdering his friend Deagol to first take the ring. Is grace yet possible for him, such that we might even say he is "saved" because, after all, he is the one who destroys the ring?

Significantly, it is Frodo who most makes us consider this point by telling Sam, in the chapter's last paragraph, "Let us forgive him." If these hobbits, who have so directly suffered because of Gollum's actions, can forgive him, maybe God can also? To hope so does not require universalism, but in his letters to readers Tolkien cautions against expecting Gollum's salvation, arguing that it is "Goddes privitee," the medieval conception of God's private judgement.[9] Certainly Frodo is wrong about "being here, at the end of all things" with Sam, and the remainder of the novel's many consolations remind us that God alone determines the conclusion of any story. Yet so closely is pity and mercy connected to March 25, the Catholic Feast of the Annunciation which began the Incarnation, that to also participate

---

9. Tolkien, *Letters*, 340.

in it by thanking Gollum for the destruction of the ring, on March 25 in Tolkien's history of Middle-earth, seems an application open to both hobbits and humans.

4. THE FIELD OF CORMALLEN: "LIKE SPRING AFTER WINTER"

The fearsome sense of finality at the end of Mount Doom is enhanced by the coming cry of the Nazgûl, and especially in Jackson's film the action happens so quickly that one wonders what happened, and whether all the "happy endings" that follow are silly attempts at box-office feel good. In the novel, this key chapter clarifies the consolation, helping readers recover Tolkien's meaning. Narrative technique is critical here, as suddenly the plots of Books V and VI are back together, and key moments, on both fronts, are at this time clarified by the "rest of the story," the moment after the intense drama we have seen.

We hear again, for example, Frodo's famous line on "the end of all things," but in this chapter Sam replies, ever hopeful, that "coming all that way I don't want to give up yet. It's not like me, somehow, if you understand." By this point Frodo, and most readers, certainly do understand, so with their "last strength of mind and body" the two friends move "slowly down the winding road" away from the cracks of doom, and are soon picked up not by Nazgûl, but instead by eagles. It is easy to dismiss these eagles as a childish "natural" form of *deus ex machina* that procures a happy ending to preserve a means to gain a happy ending. However, eagles make similar appearances elsewhere in Tolkien, and have a very defined symbolic significance in his legendarium.

Hence this chapter opens with the ending of Book V, as Aragorn stands "beneath his banner . . . his eyes gleaming like stars that shine the brighter as the night deepens." Always behind him, and in many ways the true leader, is Gandalf, "white and cold and no shadow fell on him." We hear again the cry that closed Book V, "the eagles are coming," but perhaps only Gandalf at first understands their real significance. He, after all, was rescued from Saruman by the same chief eagle who comes here, Gwaihir the Windlord, whom he now greets as "friend." Gandalf's ancient identity as "Olórin," servant to the Ainur, may also be important here as the narrator tells us that Gwaihir is descended from "old Thorondor," the eagle who rescued Beren and Lúthien from the dungeons of Melkor.

RECOVERING CONSOLATION

Most readers will also recall that eagles came to Bilbo's rescue in *The Hobbit*, but *The Silmarillion* makes especially clear that, for Tolkien, eagles are not "cheap" means of happy ending, but symbolic of divine providential power that allows the consolation essential to eucatastrophe. Jackson's film includes the defensible action of Gandalf riding an eagle to pick up Sam and Frodo from Mount Doom, but Tolkien's full theological aesthetic is surely more profound. Put in terms outside of Tolkien's literary genre, only God could save Frodo and Sam after Mount Doom, and the good news is that God chooses to do so. There is a scriptural verse behind this image, being "lifted up on eagles' wings" in Psalm 49, but the many consolations recovered in the remainder of Book VI are particular to the long story Tolkien is telling.

This chapter also helps us understand why the destruction of the ring allows Gandalf to announce: "The realm of Sauron is ended!" This is not, as casual fans of recent superhero movies might assume, because Sauron's super-powered weapon is destroyed. Rather, rejection of the Ring through free will, which all its enemies practiced in one way or another, like the fully free will that allows Mary to bear the Incarnation, means the end of the illusion of evil to control anyone's will. Sauron's spirit becomes "impotent": "A great wind took it, and it was all blown away, and passed." As for Sauron's servants, they become like ants whose leader is killed; they "wander witless and purposely and then feebly die." Sam in this chapter is honored as one of the "ringbearers" who have destroyed the ring, but it is through other words of Sam that we most vividly celebrate the consolation, or eucatastrophe, that the destruction of Sauron's realm allows.

As much as Sam's own life has changed, he still has an almost impersonal focus on the bigger story he's been part of; let's hear, he laughs, the story of "Nine-fingered Frodo and the Ring of Doom." It is Sam's reunion with Gandalf that really brings out the language of eucatastrophe, as Sam exclaims, "Gandalf! I thought you were dead! But then I thought I was dead myself. Is everything sad going to come untrue? What's happened to the world?" Gandalf's answer, that "a great Shadow has departed," is consonant with the major symbol of evil in the novel, but the deeper nature of eucatastrophe, in Tolkien's aesthetic, is heard as Gandalf then "laughed, and the sound was like music, or like water in a parched land." For Sam, this sound "fell upon his ears like the echo of all the joys he had ever known." Initially Sam "burst into tears," but then his own "laughter welled up, and laughing he sprang up" to give what to my mind is the most eloquent account of eucatastrophe:

> "How do I feel?" he cried. "Well, I don't know how to say it. I feel, I feel"—he waved his arms in the air—"I feel like spring after winter, and sun on the leaves; and like trumpets and harps and all the songs I have ever heard!" He stopped and he turned towards his master. "But how's Mr. Frodo?" he said. "Isn't it a shame about his poor hand? But I hope he's all right otherwise. He's had a cruel time."

Sam's concern for Frodo first, evident throughout the novel, is clear even here in a moment of supreme personal happiness. When a minstrel of Gondor begins singing the tale of Frodo, Sam can finally say, "All my wishes have come true!" and then weep for joy. Tolkien himself says, "I remember blotting the pages with tears" as he wrote this passage.[10] As Gandalf will say at the novel's end, "Not all tears are evil."

We don't hear much more from Sam in this great chapter, but his joy is furthered by the return of some great gifts (such as the phial and gardener's box from Galadriel) and reunions with other old friends. "Strider" responds to his former lowly name by honoring Sam, though he cannot resist reminding him: "It is a long way, is it not, from Bree, where you did not like the look of me?" Further humor comes at his reunion with Pippen and Merry, where the youngest, silliest hobbit reminds Sam that he and Merry "are knights of the City and of the Mark, as I hope you observe." Sam can't help but notice how both have grown, though he must admit that what exactly "ent-draughts" are "beats me."

Sam must especially enjoy Legolas's Elvish song of the sea, and we hear more eucatastrophe when Gimli tells us that upon finding Pippen beneath the troll, "I made sure that you were dead." Sam does not seem to recall his similar error with Frodo, though he does count it "a sad loss" when he hears that other "oliphaunts" died in the great final battle with Sauron. Ever commonsensical, Sam concludes, "Well, one can't be everywhere at once, I suppose." Even readers like myself, who mainly follow Sam's path in the novel, must agree that great good has also come through Books III and V in the novel, and more consolations related to its plots follow in the chapters yet to come in Book VI. The way in which all these stories are hallowed by God's story must fill one with laughter, and tears, as the consolation of eucatastrophe is recovered.

10. Tolkien, *Letters*, 454.

5. THE STEWARD AND THE KING: "I WOULD DEARLY LOVE TO SEE BYWATER AGAIN, AND ROSIE COTTON AND HER BROTHERS, AND THE GAFFER AND MARIGOLD AND ALL"

Though both plots are crucial in the novel, and we can certainly say that both the previous chapter and novel as a whole give much attention to Sam, it is still a bit jarring when he does not appear at all in this chapter. Thus it is not possible for my own chapter titles to continue quoting Sam from this chapter, but I have instead chosen words from the "Mount Doom" chapter because they illustrate something that is counterintuitive for most modern readers: the more important a romantic relationship is in the story, the less Tolkien focuses attention on it.

This chapter illustrates this point perfectly as the marriage we have long been waiting for, between the human-king Aragorn and the elf-queen Arwen, is recounted in just three paragraphs at the end of the chapter. Despite this chapter's title's simple balanced clause, its almost exclusive focus is on the Steward, Faramir, and the women he will marry, Éowyn. This focus does allow Tolkien to skillfully practice something very rare in his writing, a psychologically realistic romance, and most readers are very interested in Tolkien's fascinating development of two of the novel's most important characters. But no one could say that Faramir and Éowyn are a more important couple than Aragorn and Arwen. Perhaps then it is not impertinent, though it is always key to Sam's character that he is a humble servant of greatness, to reflect for a moment on why Sam's love for Rosie Cotton, expressed so clearly at Mount Doom when it appears he will never fulfill it, is for Tolkien, as clarified by the letter quoted as an epigraph in my preface, such an important part of why Sam could be regarded as the "chief hero" of the novel.

Sam to Rosie, as he bounces their first daughter Elanor on his lap, is the real final word of this novel, but to understand why this is no aesthetic accident requires insight into Tolkien's values. For few modern readers would find the passage quoted in my chapter title here as especially romantic; who puts one's beloved in the same sentence, let alone clause, as her "brothers"? Yet family only comes, in human life, through romantic love, and Sam's lament for both in the moment of his apparent death and sacrifice is a reminder of what he holds most dear. Sam's authentic emotions often can be expressed only in tears, but his real love for Rosie, and for family, is fully shown, within Tolkien's aesthetic, both in the novel proper and in its appendices, where we further learn that Sam and Rosie have several more children as he becomes the Shire mayor for the next 50 years. The romantic love of Sam for Rosie is not something extrinsic to the plot, but rather so intrinsically sacred that it can hardly be discussed, even though its fruits are manifold.

6. MANY PARTINGS: "I WISH I WAS GOING BACK TO LÓRIEN!"

Sam also does not appear very often in the next two chapters. Tolkien's choice here is required by Sam's character as a humble, selfless, sometimes almost comically simple servant, though Sam's role in the destruction of the ring certainly continues to be honored. But Tolkien is tying up many plot elements in these chapters, allowing readers to have one final glimpse of favorite characters. There are many touching moments as these characters say farewell, and some fascinating suggestions as to how the eucatastrophe of the ring will affect these characters in the future. Many of the characters were met in the books where Sam was occupied elsewhere, and one might imagine they are more important or at least more important than Sam, but he too has some memorable moments consonant with Sam's importance in the rest of the novel.

Frodo and Sam here again "rode at Aragorn's side," but often it is the minor characters who grab our attention. Arwen, for example, has perhaps her longest speaking part in the novel, as she explains to Frodo why he can have her seat on the voyage to Valinor (which begins to be foreshadowed) because she has made "the choice of Lúthien," one of the novel's few references to Elvish-human marriages that are so important in Tolkien's legendarium. It is moving to see Aragorn and Éowyn reconcile, after their earlier tension, with the king approving her marriage to Faramir in a personal way: "It heals my heart to see thee now in bliss."

Treebeard also reappears, and we learn of the valuable role Ents did play in helping the Riders of Rohan get to the final battle with Sauron. Yet Treebeard's power, like Bomabadil's, is not exaggerated or idealized; we also learn that Saruman has beguiled Treebeard and escaped Isengard. The heart of Treebeard still seems wounded, lamenting the still lost "ent-wives." Yet Treebeard shares one last ent-draught with Merry and Pippen with its much simpler friendship: they "laughed and drained their bowls."

RECOVERING CONSOLATION

Much less friendly is Gandalf's meeting with Saruman and Wormtongue. All three remain bitter enemies, for whom friendship is only an outward show. Despite being amongst the most intelligent and craftiest characters in the novel, in obvious contrast to "simple Sam," the villains here are seemingly not yet touched by eucatastrophe. Not even Gandalf has the wisdom to reconcile them, though it is striking how he grants even these evil-doers free will and an extended "moment" of choice. Again, application to the divine treatment of fallen humanity seems obvious.

Sam and all of the hobbits are disturbed by Saruman's suggestions of trouble back in the shire. Sam had a vision, in the mirror of Galadriel, of the Shire uprooted and his "Gaffer," especially, in trouble. Sam here wonders how Saruman "bought" tobacco from the Shire, and "didn't like the sound of what he said about the Southfarthing." "It's time we got back," Sam concludes, but then arrives perhaps his favorite single character from the entire quest: Galadriel, with her husband Celeborn. As Galadriel held her ring aloft, one of the three Elven rings still creating beauty and untouched by Sauron, it is "a token of farewell." Seeming to forget all he has said about Rosie Cotton or his Gaffer, Sam blurts out: "I wish I was going back to Lórien!"

Clearly this is an emotional outburst, but Tolkien regards it of sufficient importance to write it as a single paragraph. Sam truly loved seeing the Elves, and when their farewell journey arrives back in Rivendell, Sam gives a fuller commentary:

> Well, Mr. Frodo, we've been far and seen a deal, and yet I don't think we've found a better place than this. There's something of everything here, if you understand me: the Shire and the Golden Wood and Gondor and kings' houses and inns and meadows and mountains all mixed. And yet, somehow, I feel we ought to be going soon. I'm worried about my gaffer, to tell you the truth.

Sam's love for the Elves is very clear, but it is also clear that his love for his "gaffer," and for the Shire more generally, will send him home. Frodo, by contrast, is here already longing for "the sea."

Rivendell allows a final meeting with beloved Bilbo, who without the anti-aging power of the ring was too weak to travel to Gondor. Aragorn and Arwen's wedding is the part of the whole quest that most interests Bilbo, but the adventurous old man redirects this interest to Sam, giving him "a little bag of gold," left over from Smaug's hoard. It "may come in useful, if you decide to marry, Sam," Bilbo explains. "Sam blushed," but of course does not mention Rosie Cotton.

Bilbo then specifically questions Sam about the oliphaunt, asking, "Did you really see one?" before singing, one last time, the old walking song that has proven so profound, "The Road goes ever on and on." Finally Bilbo suggests Sam as an aide to Frodo writing down this long story. When the chapter closes with a final suggestion that Frodo will not be long for the Shire, the crucial future role of Sam as storyteller, long suggested by his enchantment with the Elves, now becomes clear. Sam's role as ringbearer was shared with Bilbo and Frodo, but it is from the older hobbit that Sam first gained his love for stories that really matter.

7. HOMEWARD BOUND: "ANOTHER WISH COME TRUE"

As readers, then, we have a special gratitude for Sam returning to the Shire. On the way there, this chapter stops again in Bree, the place where the hobbits had their first crucial meeting with Aragorn. Sam turns the king's joke on him onto the kind-hearted but almost comically naïve innkeeper at Bree, "Barliman Butterbur." "Strider," Sam says, is "of course" the new king; "Haven't you gotten that into your head?" Sam is comically but almost arrogantly interrogating Butterbur, which could annoy but should remind us of Sam's errors the last time he was in Bree.

A comic moment also brings us back to that time, as the hobbits arrive at the home of "Bill Ferny" and Pippen asks, "Do you think you killed him with that apple, Sam?" "I'm not so hopeful," Sam says, a reply that might lower our sense of his sublime role in returning hope to Middle-earth. Yet Sam's honest, realistic love is for a companion who could not complete the journey. Recalling the pony left outside Moria, Sam adds: "I'd like to know what became of that poor pony. He's been on my mind many a time and the wolves howling and all." In this chapter, both Sam and the novel's readers learn the truth.

Unfazed by Sam's tone, the amazed Butterbur replies, "Strider . . . with a crown and all and a golden cup," but the really important thing he says to Sam is, "I've something that belongs to you." His reference is to "Bill," the pony Sam saved from "Bill Ferny." Sam reacts emotionally, reminding us of his anguish after losing the pony outside of Moria. "What! My Bill?" Sam cried, and then adds a comment which suggests the great importance of

Recovering Consolation

this seemingly minor plot element: "There's another wish come true!" Sam does not go to bed, even tired after his long journey, "until he had visited Bill in his stable." Later in the chapter, we see Bill reciprocate the emotion. "Bill the Pony" is "with them," and particularly he "trotted along beside Sam and seemed well content."

Sam cannot help but think, as the chapter closes, of his "old Gaffer" and how he should have "hurried back quicker" after seeing the mirror of Galadriel. Yet readers know that Sam has been travelling on God's schedule. Real hope depends on seeing history as God does rather than through human means, even the beautiful objects of art. Perhaps this is why this chapter's conclusion gives the fascinating moment when Gandalf turns aside to go talk with Tom Bombadil, explaining:

> I am going to have a long talk with Bombadil: such a talk as I have not had in all my time. He is a moss-gatherer, and I have been a stone doomed to rolling. But my rolling days are ending, and now we shall have much to say to one another.

This is a conversation that every reader of Tolkien would want to hear. But *The Lord of the Rings* does not give us any of it, closing instead with Sam's words to Rosie and Elanor. To understand why, we too must return to the Shire, and see the normal family's real need for sanctity. Sam never teaches us this in a sanctimonious way, but his example does allow laughter, and recovery of the profound consolation of eucatastrophe.

8. THE SCOURING OF THE SHIRE: "IT IS HOME"

Readers have to be pleased that Sam is going home to the Shire, rather than Lórien, if only in anticipation of his reunion with Rosie Cotton and his "Gaffer." We do get to set this here, but most of this chapter is a cleanup of evil that has creeped into the Shire during Sauron's realm. All four of the original fellowship of hobbit friends are present throughout, though Merry and, to a lesser extent Pippen, play the leading roles, almost balancing the conclusion in a manner similar to how the plot is divided in the novel as a whole.

Sam does get the last word, however, and the first words in the chapter, when the hobbit-friends arrive in the Shire and discover it has been taken over by scurrilous authorities and silly rules. Sam's satiric, comic, and even violent tendencies come out; asked to read a "notice," he shouts, "Of course we can't read the notice in the dark. . . . And if hobbits of the Shire are to be kept out in the wet on a night like this, I'll tear down your notice when I find it." It is Merry and Pippen who first "climbed the gate" to enter, but when "Bill Ferny" is found inside, it is a swift kick from "Bill," Sam's pony, that sends this villain running away, "never heard of again"; "'Neat work, Bill,' said Sam, meaning the pony." Much needs to be done in the Shire, but after summarizing its problems Sam has the same common sense that sustained him during the long quest to destroy the ring: "Let's sleep and forget it till morning."

If anything, Sam must give way to Merry in this task so that cooler heads can prevail. Sam is infuriated by the new Shire "shirriff," and asks to be arrested for "Calling your Chief Names, Wishing to Punch His Pimple Face, and Thinking you Shirrifs look a lot of Tom-Fools." Sam's real sympathy for even these fools does come out, though, in conversation with one new "shirriff," Robin Smallburrow. Sam will meet him at the Green Dragon Inn after all the nonsense has ended; this is where we first heard Sam speak in the novel, and in this chapter Sam must also again engage his interlocutor there, Ted Sandyman, and discover sadly that his nature has not really changed. Yet perhaps most significantly of all, Sam and Frodo recognize the Shire as their "own country," and remember "that they cared about it more than any other place in the world."

As Merry rationally plans the trap that will ensnare the Shire "ruffians" and ensure minimal loss of hobbit lives (Frodo's main concern), Sam plots how to visit the Cotton family. We know he is going to see Rosie, but her first words to him are not deeply romantic: "Hullo, Sam! . . . Where've you been? They said you were dead; but I've been expecting you since the spring. You haven't hurried, have you?" There is a hint of the eucatastrophic spirit so prevalent since the destruction of the ring, but an even greater suggestion that Sam is a bit late getting back to see her. Even more direct undercutting of the honor and praise given to Sam immediately after Mount Doom comes when we finally hear live words of the oft-quoted Gaffer. When we first see him with his son, "Old Gamgee" addresses Frodo:

> "Good evening, Mr. Baggins!" he said. "Glad indeed I am to see you safe back. But I've a bone to pick with you, in a manner o' speaking, if I may make so bold. You didn't never ought to have a' sold Bag End, as I always said. That's what started all the mischief. And while you've been trapessing in foreign parts, chasing Black Men up mountains from what my Sam says, though what for he

don't make clear, they've been and dug up Bagshot Row and ruined my taters!"

One can at least be sure that Sam has come honestly by his love of "taters," but also be tempted to critique both Rosie and Sam's father as backwards, provincial, for not recognizing the significance of Sauron's defeat, and Sam's important role in this defeat. Most of all, though, we should be thankful for the natural humility of Sam's family, which likely is the key factor in making him the loving servant that he is. Tellingly, Tolkien has Frodo, the person who has benefitted most directly from this service, defend Sam, telling his Gaffer: "Indeed, if you will believe it, he's now one of the most famous people in all the lands, and they are making songs about his deeds from here to the Sea and beyond the Great River." Sam "blushed," as so often before, but "Rosie's eyes were shining, and she was smiling at him."

A far more difficult conversation awaits Sam when he again meets Ted Sandyman, who had ridiculed Sam back when we first met him. They meet just after Sam and Frodo have just had "one of the saddest hours of their life," seeing every tree felled along Bywater Road, a sight that not "even Sam's vision in the Mirror" of Galadriel had prepared him to see. Even the "Party Tree," under which Bilbo had given his "farewell" speech to the Shire, has been cut down.

Ted, working now for the Shire's new political regime, mercilessly rubs this loss in Sam's face: "Don't 'ee like it Sam? . . . But you always was soft." Completely unaware of all that has gone on in Middle-earth since the first conversation we heard him have with Sam, Sandyman is still mocking Elves: "I thought you'd gone off in one o' them ships you used to prattle about, sailing, sailing. What d'you want to come back for? We've work to do in the Shire now." In reply, Sam wittily mocks both Ted's work ethic and cleanliness, noting that Ted has "no time for washing," but has "time for wall-propping." He has bigger things on his mind now, and is unwilling to spend much time on the moronic: "But see here, Master Sandyman, I've a score to pay in this village, and don't you make it any longer with your jeering, or you'll foot a bill too big for your purse." Sam's heart-felt response, though, comes just after, with Frodo, the one person now who truly knows where Sam has been: "This is worse than Mordor!" said Sam. "Much worse in a way. It comes home to you, as they say; because it is home, and you remember it before it was all ruined."

When the hobbits meet the "Boss" that Ted is working for, who has gone by the apt name "Sharkey," this tyrant's real identity as Saruman is

BOOK SIX

soon revealed. Frodo follows Gandalf in offering mercy, even at this stage, but Saruman's response reminds us of the ring-wraiths at Weathertop, passing close to Frodo before flashing a knife and stabbing swiftly. One last time the "mail-coat" of Bilbo saves Frodo, and readers see one more time when Sam will join the two other hobbits in putting on the armor of mercy. Frodo counsels:

> "No, Sam!" said Frodo. "Do not kill him even now. For he has not hurt me. And in any case I do not wish him to be slain in this evil mood. He was great once, of a noble kind that we should not dare to raise our hands against. He is fallen, and his cure is beyond us; but I would still spare him, in the hope that he may find it."

Saruman's response is predictable, and directly addressed to Frodo, but we can apply it also to Sam:

> Saruman rose to his feet, and stared at Frodo. There was a strange look in his eyes of mingled wonder and respect and hatred. "You have grown, Halfling," he said. "Yes, you have grown very much. You are wise, and cruel. You have robbed my revenge of sweetness, and now I must go hence in bitterness, in debt to your mercy. I hate it and you! Well, I go and I will trouble you no more. But do not expect me to wish you health and long life. You will have neither. But that is not my doing. I merely foretell."

Sam, unlike the wounded Frodo, will have "health and long life," but not because of any power still in Saruman. Rather, the hobbits' pity has robbed evil of any power to further revenge. As with Gollum, the mercy shown here to Saruman can seem irrational and extreme, but it does finally end the cycle of violence which Sauron's realm fostered.

The actual execution of Saruman is performed, however, by someone perhaps even more devoted to evil than the villains we've come to know in the novel so far. "Wormtongue" has followed Saruman from Isengard, but here snaps after "Sharkey" blames him for the murder of innocent hobbits like Lotho Baggins, then "kicked [him] in the face." Wormtongue stabs Saruman before being felled himself by hobbit arrows. Sam gives the commonsensical commentary: "And that's the end of that. A nasty end, and I wish I needn't have seen it; but it's a good riddance." Merry gives the broader view, calling it "the very last end of the War," and Frodo concurs, hoping that it is "the very last stroke."

Frodo cannot also help but add the ironic note that makes this long, often painful return to the Shire necessary both in the hobbits' lives and in

Recovering Consolation

the novel itself: "But to think that it should fall here, at the very door of Bag End! Among all my hopes and fears at least I never expected that." Sam, though, has learned through the eucatastrophe of Mount Doom that it is not his role to proclaim or announce end times. This falls to God, and so Sam has a simpler, humbler, and more realistic way to conclude the scouring of the Shire: "I shan't call it the end, till we've cleared up the mess. And that'll take a lot of time and work."

In the next chapter, which is truly the novel's end—but by no means the end of Tolkien's *legendarium*, which the novel's appendices stretch far into the future—we shall see how Sam's concept of "time and work" is fundamentally different than Ted Sandyman's, because Sam has learned the immortal beauty of the Elvish world.

9. THE GREY HAVENS: "WELL, I'M BACK"

As already noted, this final chapter will also conclude with words from Sam, words that again affirm him coming home, but the meaning of those words is much enhanced through the often poetic Elvish themes and events of this final chapter. Whereas "the scouring of the Shire" is almost a mini novella of prose set entirely in the Shire, "the Grey Havens" is a reminder of the much broader epic that is Tolkien's entire *legendarium*. This final chapter begins on an optimistic note, as the work to clean up the shire "took less time than Sam had feared." Demolition of the lockholes, after the liberation of its prisoners, gives tragi-comic glimpses of some old friends, and enemies: "Fatty Bulgar" is considerably slimmer, and Pippen cannot resist needling him. We feel true pity, though, even for Lobelia, who upon her release returns Bag End to Frodo and, after her death, wills the rest of his estate to homeless hobbits. Thus another "feud is ended."

Sam is "very busy" in the reconstruction of the Shire, especially with the numerous trees destroyed, as in Fangorn, because of Saruman's mischief. Perhaps he is too re-immersed in Shire life to think of it earlier, but "suddenly one day . . . he remembered the gift of Galadriel," the "gardener's box," and its seeds, by the next spring, had "surpassed his wildest hopes." Yet as with the other "magic" in the story, Tolkien makes clear that the power of the "gardener's box" is not independent or strictly supernatural. Frodo tells Sam, "Use all the wits and knowledge you have of your own, Sam . . . and then use the gift to help your work and better it." As so often in Tolkien, free will cooperates with grace to bring forth abundant fruit. In this case, trees sprout all over, but replacing the "Party Tree" of Bilbo is now a "mallorn," as grew in Lothlórien: "The only mallorn west of the Mountains and east of the Sea, and one of the finest in the world."

Galadriel's beautiful forest has one last gift for Sam, maybe the most precious of all. Sam marries Rosie in the spring of that year (1420, an exceptionally abundant year, in all ways, in the Shire), and the ongoing eucatastrophe of the Ring is especially shown the following spring, when on March 25 ("a date that Sam noted") the first child of Sam and Rosie is born. If male they would name him Frodo, but when the child is female Frodo thinks, "Well, Sam, what about *elanor*, the sun-star, you remember the little golden flower in the grass of Lothlórien?" Sam is delighted and his response reminds us of how providence, and the wisdom of his friends, so often combine to fulfill his true deepest wishes: "That's what I wanted."

Sam is truly conflicted about one thing. He can't help but notice and be upset by the pain that Frodo often feels, the deep pain of wounds that make him more fit for Valinor than the Shire. Sam is also "pained to notice how little honour [Frodo] had in his own country," but what has really "torn in two" Sam is the conflict between being with Frodo and living the busy life of a happily married hobbit. Again, Frodo's wisdom is key: "Do not be too sad, Sam. You cannot be always torn in two. You will have to be one, and whole, for many years. You have so much to enjoy and to be and do." In Jackson's film, these words become "voice-over" that stresses Sam's importance at the end of the journey. In Tolkien's novel, just how much Sam will do is fully described in the index, where we learn that Sam will be the Shire mayor for fifty years and have many more children with Rosie. A sneak preview of these children, and their names, is in this final chapter given by the prophetic Frodo, who adds that Sam will become "the most famous gardener in history." Frodo, as Bilbo requested, also passes along to Sam the "red book" of all their adventures, saying, "I have quite finished, Sam . . . the last pages are for you."

Frodo does note, as they are about to depart for the grey havens, the harbor where Cirdan the Shipwright ferries Elves back to Valinor, that "you too were a Ring-Bearer," and though Sam will not be on this voyage, "your time may come." The appendix confirms that Sam does follow Frodo to Valinor after Rosie's death at the end of his life, but for now Sam must be content with a last glimpse of Elrond and Galadriel, now openly wearing their Elvish rings. Galadriel commends his work with the Shire's trees:

Recovering Consolation

"Well, Master Samwise . . . I hear and see that you have used my gift well. The Shire shall now be more than ever blessed and beautiful."

For once, Sam "found nothing to say," but perhaps this is the surest sign that he is again deeply moved by "how beautiful the Lady was." This final glimpse of Elvish magic, combined with Frodo's farewell, gives Sam "a sadness that was yet blessed and without bitterness," but as ever his spirit is lifted by his friends: "Up rode Merry and Pippen in great haste. And amid his tears Pippen laughed." If any readers yet miss the consolation, Gandalf's wisdom spells it out one last time: "Go in peace! I will not say: do not weep; for not all tears are an evil." Gandalf too wears an elf-ring as he speaks, but even greater consolation awaits Sam at home.

In a sense, this consolation is specifically contrasted to the Elvish. As Frodo sails off into "his dream in the house of Bombadil, the grey rain-curtain turned all to silver glass," whereas for Sam "the evening deepened to darkness." Yet as Sam rides home in silence with Merry and Pippen, "each had great comfort in his friends on the long grey road," and upon reaching home there is an even greater comfort: "Rose drew him in, and set him in his chair, and put little Elanor upon his lap." This simple domestic scene, after all the adventure, then concludes this epic novel with one of the simplest lines in all of English literature: "He drew a deep breath. 'Well, I'm back,' he said."

An English professor could offer a word-by-word analysis of the novel's great conclusion. Yet on a supra-intellectual, even transcendent level, we can feel recovery of the basic goodness of breathing, and the "whole" return of Sam to the consolation intended for his identity by the Meaner who made him. Eucatastrophe awaits!

Conclusion
A Sanctified Hobbit-Hero

BY THE END OF our journey, most readers will recognize Samwise Gamgee as, in some sense, a hero. Some readers might even see him as, in some sense, sanctified. But in what sense is either term really significant? To return to the epitaph from Tolkien's letters with which I began, in what sense can we see Sam as the novel's "chief hero"?[1] Can we, as human readers, have any grasp of the consolation offered by Sam's inner life, given that he is a sanctified hobbit hero rather than a human leader of any kind?

We must approach such questions humbly, given that even his closest friends are often surprised by Sam. We recall, for example, Sam's long poem about Bombadil, when Merry remarked, "There's more stored in your head than you let on about," and Pippen asked, "Where did you come by that, Sam?" Sam's own answer was "inaudible," though scholars are likely quick to answer, "Tolkien himself," given that Sam's poem does appear in a collection, *The Adventures of Tom Bombadil*, that Tolkien published after *The Lord of the Rings*. We have often seen how Sam's attitude to Elves echoes Tolkien's aesthetic, how Sam's recovery of consolation leads to enchantment and prepares us to enjoy eucatastrophe. Yet can we really share this vision, especially as moderns typically proud of our heads and often out of touch with our hearts?

We must humbly acknowledge this difficulty, but Tolkien does make Sam, surely as much as any character in his epic, one who stays "in the heart" of anyone willing to listen to his comical yet often complex words. Sam's unusual aptitude for the Elvish, perhaps best shown by the perceptive comment on Bombadil's unique nature that we noted back in chapter 7 of Book I, is expressed often in the novel. Those who underestimate Sam,

1. Tolkien, *Letters*, 229.

dismissing him as an unlearned servant, are likely to miss the profundity of this character. As noted, Sam's direct reply to one of the central cruxes of Tolkien Studies, the identity of Bombadil, is rarely cited, and so far very few books have focused mainly on Sam's character.

This tendency to underestimate Sam is perhaps even greater for those who know him mainly from Jackson's films rather than Tolkien's novel. Sean Astin's portrayal of Sam is excellent, and Jackson's casting choices are usually superb. Yet the problem is not simply the condensed nature of film, which forces omission of many events in the novel. The greater problem is how material enactments can portray interior spiritual complexity. Some of Jackson's choices with the ring, stressing its dangerous effects rather than Tolkien's more varied treatment of its effect on Bombadil or Sam, are probably due to a desire not to confuse an unlearned popular audience, perhaps unlikely to understand that the ring is a highly complex form of evil.

Sam's enchanted interior life is also greatly simplified, however, which could be taken as one more example of the superiority of literature over film. C. S. Lewis, Tolkien's fellow "Inkling," once said in a letter that he opposed Narnia becoming film because "when taken out of narrative into actual visibility," it "always turns into buffoonery or nightmare."[2] Tolkien makes a similar statement in "On Fairy-Stories," arguing that drama is a material form unsuited to the "fantasy" genre in which he prefers to write.[3] As modes such as the soliloquy can temper this aspect of drama, however, so it should be possible to "show" more of Sam's Elvish enchantment. Jackson's film has Sam saving Frodo from the orc tower by "stick" of sword through the back, but Tolkien's much more complex treatment at the end of Book VI and beginning of Book IV shows Sam's reliance on the Elvish and resistance to the ring because of the powerful interior love he has for Frodo. Tolkien's Sam is certainly no pacifist, and he does cut off the "whip-hand" of the orc left to guard Frodo, Snaga, after the infighting between the orc leaders, Shagrat and Gorbac, drive both away.

Those without any taste of Elvish enchantment may find Jackson's Sam more heroic than Tolkien's, but Sam's enchanted inner life is a key part of what is recovered in the journey, as Jackson himself seems to recognize by returning to Tolkien's focus upon Sam at the end of *The Return of the King*. The consolations given to Sam are surely concrete, especially Rosie Cotton (as Sam would likely be the first to point out), but it is crucial to recognize

---

2. Lewis, *Narnia, Cambridge, and Joy*, 1111.
3. Tolkien, "On Fairy-Stories," 50.

CONCLUSION

that in Tolkien's Elvish aesthetic the material and spiritual are not opposed. Rather, the real meaning of "stone, and wood, and iron," is recovered, not through definition or dissection but rather "wonder."[4] Perhaps the clearest path Tolkien gives for us to understand this is the stars. So much of the Elvish in Tolkien comes from the stars, and even in Mordor it is "the beauty" of the star rising above shadow that "smote [Sam's] heart."

Tolkien's poem "Mythopoeia" can also help us. An address from "Philomythus" (lover of myth) to "Misomythus" (hater of myth) this extraordinary poem, also published in *Tree and Leaf*, starts by mocking material empiricists for whom "a star's a star, some matter in a ball" (line 5), but eventually offers the Elvish poetry and song that Sam so loves:

> He sees no stars who does not see them first
> of living silver made that sudden burst
> to flame like flower beneath an ancient song,
> whose very echo after-music long
> has since pursued. (lines 45–49)

Beauty here has a power that many find difficult to relate to the very explicit Catholic theology that one finds, for example, in Tolkien's epilogue to "On Fairy-Stories." Here again we are aided by broad consideration of Tolkien's *legendarium*. Yet simple Sam is the fullest embodiment of what Tolkien means by "hobbito-centric," the "ennoblement (or sanctification) of the humble."[5] We cannot call him a saint, but the "sanctification" of his interior life can be related to Catholic concepts of the holy, the English for the Latin "sanctus." Prior to philology, though, understanding Tolkien's Sam perhaps requires, first, some sense of why it is so difficult for any human to become convinced of credible sanctity. We easily dismiss most claims to sanctity as "sanctimonious," power-seeking posturing to establish what Lear calls "the image of authority"[6] rather than any holy reality to be believed let alone obeyed. For many people, any sense of sanctity is lost in childhood, when a religious leader's sanctity is revealed to be, at best, hypocrisy.

If not others' sins, then our own sin inwardly convicts us, even if this is too painful to admit. Without question, as every Catholic knows, we need a Holy Savior. Thankfully, we have One. Any God truly believed in must be holy, amongst all of the logically necessary attributes of divinity, but Catholicism especially strives to develop some sense of the holy. The

---

4. Tolkien, "On Fairy-Stories," 60.
5. Tolkien, *Letters*, 343.
6. Shakespeare, *King Lear*, 4.5.154.

Holy Spirit, of course, is one person of the Holy Trinity, and every Catholic sacrament is intended, as its Latin etymology insists, to be an introduction to the holy. Bernthal, in particular, has shown how much of *The Lord of the Ring's* action, imagery, and themes can be illuminated through reference to Catholic sacramental life. There is an unsurprising tendency, amongst devout Catholics, to seek sanctity only in the church, just as any Christian might ask this fundamental question: why would one read other books, already possessing the perfect text that is the Holy Bible?

Tolkien answers such questions not, like many realistic writers, by depicting fiction that clearly applies to problems common in human life. Au contraire, Tolkien develops a vast mythology usually focused on Elves, subjects that Tolkien himself, before the publication of his work, believes will be seen as irrelevant to our world. The hobbits who emerge in the "third age" of his fiction are a surprise to Tolkien, just as the elf and human races are a surprise created by Ilúvatar upon the creation of Middle-earth.

Yet if we attend closely to "Ainulindalë," the creation myth that opens *The Silmarillion*, we realize that both kinds of creatures known as "the children of Ilúvatar," Elves and human beings, reflect God's purposes beyond what can be known even by the wisest, the "Ainur" who, in Tolkien's mythology, aid in God's creation. "The Ainur know much of what was, and is, and is to come," like Galadriel and Gandalf in the Third Age, but from Ilúvatar comes "forth things that are new and have no foretelling." So when the immortal Ainur see the creation of Elves and humans, "The more did they love them, being things other than themselves, strange and free, wherein they saw the mind of Ilúvatar reflected anew, and learned a little more of his wisdom, which otherwise had been hidden even to the Ainur."[7]

Marriage between Elves and humans is another crucial surprise, and God turns the evil faced by the elf Lúthien and human hero Beren (in an especially striking "application," the names that Tolkien puts on the gravestone of he and his wife[8]) into a genealogical line that leads to Eärendil, the mariner who recovers the way to Valinor, and eventually to Elrond and his daughter Arwen, who becomes Queen in the Third Age. Tolkien's letters confirm that Beren and Lúthien are a "fundamental link" in his mythology,[9] but the rationale of this link is clarified by one of the most traditionally Catholic elements of "Ainulindalë." Ilúvatar does not

---

7. Tolkien, *Silmarillion*, 5–6.
8. See Maillet, "Meeting Somewhere in Truth."
9. Tolkien, *Letters*, 209.

CONCLUSION

simply destroy Melkor, despite all the evil he will cause, but instead turns his evil to good, explicitly telling us, just before revelation of the unforeseen "children," that Melkor "wilt discover all the secret parts of my mind, and wilt perceive that they are but a part of the whole and tributary to its glory."

As part of the same story, in a world governed by the same God, and aware that hobbits themselves are a surprise to their creator, Tolkien, we can explore further what might be meant by calling Sam a "hero." One must be more precise than to claim him as the leading character of the novel, for this claim vainly competes against Gandalf, Frodo, even Gollum. Samwise Gamgee becomes an exceptionally important hobbit, and character in Tolkien's legendarium, by combining an honest, simple, child-like interest in Elves with all the best qualities of the finest hobbits: humble, comical, loyal, with large doses of the surprising courage that hobbits are known to find in a tough spot.

We have noted Wood's claim that Sam is an "ultimate hero" because he is an "ultimate servant," and certainly the high value accorded to servants in Christianity can be applied to Sam, especially for Catholics who understand that a Pope must be, as several great popes have shown, a servant of the servants of God. Yet we have also noted that Tolkien deliberately highlights Sam's flaws so perhaps, though not in as obvious or extreme manner as Gollum, Sam's heroism is fully shown by how Ilúvatar brings good from Sam not only *despite* these flaws, but even *because* of them. In the eventual distance and peace offered by Elvish light, we know that Sam is ultimately not in Gollum's hands, but rather God's loving embrace and firm grip.

The part of the novel that most clearly illustrates this is surely the end of Book IV, where Sam almost concludes that Frodo has been killed by Shelob's sting and almost leaves him to the orcs and carries on the quest alone. "You fool," Sam admonishes himself, "He isn't dead, and your heart knew it. Don't trust your head, Samwise, it is not the best part of you." It was perfectly logical and rational to conclude that Frodo was dead, and that he must destroy the ring alone, but it wasn't *true*. Nor can we romantically claim that it was Sam's interior life, spirit, soul, or whatever synonym might be given here for "heart," which correctly perceived that Frodo was alive. Much more prosaically, but realistically, Sam learns this key truth by overhearing the evil orcs arguing with themselves. What does come from Sam's inner life is his clear sense of moral duty: "Never leave your master, never, never: that was my right rule. And I knew it in my heart. May I be forgiven!"

Recovering Consolation

With this clarity, which comes just a chapter after the discourse on stories at "The Stair of Cirith Ungol," we see clearly why the tales that "really matter" concern heroes who don't know whether they are in a sad or happy tale; such heroes have many chances to turn back, as Sam says then soon illustrates, but their courageous will allows them to go forward. We readily concur with Frodo's assessment on the stairs of Cirith Ungol, that "he would not have gotten far without Sam," and on the rest of the journey we see Sam making the tough choices and enduring hard suffering. By the novel's conclusion, we are fully justified in seeing Sam as a true friend to Frodo, as loving to him as Jesus was to the disciples in calling them friends, not simply servants.

Sam thus allows us to "recover," within the genre of what Tolkien means by the "fairy story," a "clear view" of the reality of sanctity.[10] This is not to claim that hobbits are models for human life, but rather that the best of them, such as Sam, and the best of Elves, or even the half-Elven, the "maiar" such as Gandalf, or the highest form human beings such as Beren, do illuminate, and thus help us to understand, part of the mind of Ilúvatar, and of the real, living God. Ilúvatar illuminates the "Light of the World," in no small part by never seeking to replace Him.

This "application" is not allegorical, but Sam does play a crucial role in the much broader recovery of consolation, the eucatastrophe, achieved by the novel as a whole. In this sense we can clearly view Sam as heroic, while retaining the wisdom of humility natural only to the small, the meek, the unheroic. Perhaps because Sam merely plays a part in this consolation, as does Frodo or Gollum, he helps us more humbly recognize that only our Lord can ever finally be the Lord of all the Rings, not just Sauron's ring, and this is the Lord who ultimately "hallows" the ending of stories, as the epilogue of Tolkien's great lecture concludes. Even Sam *needs* to humbly ask for forgiveness.

"To hallow" is an older, pre-vowel shift, way for the English to say, "make holy," but the point here cannot simply be linguistic. We must take it seriously, even cry tears of remorse, when we fall out of communion with the sanctity of our Lord. So serious can be sin that we inevitably become self-centered, and can lose a sense not only of God's holiness but of the good our Lord originally created in our original identity. We can become Gollum, debating with Sméagol. We don't see, in the novel, where that debate finally leads, nor can we say finally whether it is Frodo's pity or Sam's

---

10. Tolkien, "On Fairy-Stories," 57.

CONCLUSION

common sense that preserves the destruction of the ring. This, as Tolkien explains in his letters, is "Goddes privitee."[11] Yet rather than agonize over the ultimate destiny of Gollum's soul, or our own, Sam helps us to celebrate our Lord's sovereignty by enjoying, finding real joy, in the consolation. Sam helps us to laugh.

As with magic, one must distinguish what this laughter means. Not dismissive or satirical laughter, nor any expression of pride, but rather the laughter of Frodo, not heard in Middle-earth since Sauron's reign began. On the stairs of Cirith Ungol, the childlike voice of Frodo—for children are surely closer to hobbits than most humans—has it right: "I want to hear more of his talk, dad. He makes me laugh." Sam is a sanctified hobbit-hero, and so we all need to hear more of his talk, to which the Holy Spirit allows us to respond with a laugh of joy!

---

11. Tolkien, *Letters*, 340.

Bibliography

Alighieri, Dante. *The Divine Comedy of Dante Alighieri*. Translated by Henry Wadsworth Longfellow. London: Routledge, 1892.
Allen, Judson Boyce. *The Ethical Poetic of the Later Middle Ages*. Toronto: University of Toronto Press, 1982.
Bernthal, Craig. *Tolkien's Sacramental Vision: Discerning the Holy in Middle-earth*. Kettering, OH: Angelico, 2014.
Berry, Wendell. "How to Be a Poet." *Poetry* 177.3 (2001) 269–70.
Birzer, Bradley J. *J. R. R. Tolkien's Sanctifying Myth: Understanding Middle-earth*. Wilmington, DE: Intercollegiate Studies Institute, 2002.
Caldecott, Stratford. *The Power of the Ring: The Spiritual Vision behind "The Lord of the Rings" and "The Hobbit."* Chestnut Ridge, NY: Crossroad, 2012.
Caldecott, Stratford, and Thomas Honegger, eds. *Tolkien's "The Lord of the Rings": Sources of Inspiration*. Zollikffen, Switzerland: Walking Tree, 2008.
Carpenter, Humphrey. *J. R. R. Tolkien. A Biography*. London. Allen & Unwin, 1977.
Chance, Jane, ed. *Tolkien the Medievalist*. New York: Routledge, 2003.
Edwards, Raymond. *Tolkien*. Ramsbury, Marlborough Wiltshire, UK: Crowood, 2014.
Flieger, Verlyn. *Interrupted Music: The Making of Tolkien's Mythology*. Kent, OH: Kent State University Press, 2005.
———. *Splintered Light: Logos and Languages in Tolkien's World*. Grand Rapids: Eerdmans, 1983.
Freeman, Austin M. *Tolkien Dogmatics: Theology through Mythology with the Maker of Middle-earth*. Norfolk, UK: Lexham, 2022.
Gilliver, Peter, et al. *The Ring of Words: Tolkien and the Oxford English Dictionary*. Oxford: Oxford University Press, 2000.
Haldas, Michael C. *Echoes of Truth: Christianity in "The Lord of the Rings."* Edinburgh: Luna, 2018.
Hammond, Wayne, and Christina Scull. *"The Lord of the Rings": A Reader's Companion*. London: HarperCollins, 2014.
Hart, Trevor, and Ivan Khovacs. *Tree of Tales: Tolkien, Literature, and Theology*. Waco, TX: Baylor University Press, 2007.
Hilder, Monika B., et al. *The Inklings and Culture: A Harvest of Scholarship from the Inklings Institute of Canada*. Newcastle upon Tyne, UK: Cambridge Scholars, 2020.
Hopkins, Gerard Manley. *The Correspondence of Gerard Manley Hopkins and Richard Watson Dixon*. Edited by C. C. Abbott. Oxford: Oxford University Press, 1935.

BIBLIOGRAPHY

———. "The May Magnificat." In *Gerard Manley Hopkins: The Oxford Authors*, edited by Catherine Phillips, 139. Oxford: Oxford University Press, 1986.

Hren, Joshua. *Middle-earth and the Return of the Common Good: J. R. R. Tolkien and Political Philosophy*. Eugene, OR: Wipf & Stock, 2018.

Jackson, Peter, dir. *The Fellowship of the Ring*. DVD. Montreal, QC, Canada: Alliance Atlantis, 2002.

———. *The Return of the King*. DVD. Montreal, QC, Canada: Alliance Atlantis, 2003.

———. *The Two Towers*. DVD. Montreal, QC, Canada: Alliance Atlantis, 2002.

Kerry, Paul E. *The Ring and the Cross: Christianity and "The Lord of the Rings."* Teaneck, NJ: Fairleigh Dickinson University Press, 2010.

Kreeft, Peter. *The Philosophy of Tolkien: The Worldview behind "The Lord of the Rings."* San Francisco: Ignatius, 2005.

———. "Wartime Wisdom: Ten Uncommon Insights about Evil in *The Lord of the Rings*." In *Celebrating Middle-earth: "The Lord of the Rings" as a Defense of Western Civilization*, edited by John G. West, 31–52. Seattle, WA: Inkling, 2002.

Lewis, C. S. *Narnia, Cambridge, and Joy, 1950–1963*. The Collected Letters of C. S. Lewis 3. Edited by Walter Hooper. London: HarperCollins, 2007.

———. *Perelandra*. 1943. London: HarperCollins, 2005.

———. *A Preface to Paradise Lost*. Oxford: Oxford University Press, 1961.

Maillet, Greg. "'Meeting Somewhere in Truth': Allegory, Story, and the Significance of the Tale of Beren and Luthien." In *The Inklings and Culture: A Harvest of Scholarship from the Inklings Institute of Canada*, edited by Monika B. Hilder et al., 179–91. Newcastle upon Tyne, UK: Cambridge Scholars, 2020.

Martin, Thomas L. "God and Laughter: Overcoming the Darkness in Modern Fantasy Literature." *North Wind* 34 (2015) 4–12.

McIntosh, Jonathan S. *The Flame Imperishable: Tolkien, St. Thomas, and the Metaphysics of Faerie*. Kettering, OH: Angelico, 2017.

Milbank, Alison. *Chesterton and Tolkien as Theologians*. London: Bloomsbury T&T Clark, 2009.

O'Brien, Michael D. *The Sabbatical*. San Francisco: Ignatius, 2021.

Ordway, Holly. *Tolkien's Faith: A Spiritual Biography*. Washington, DC: Word on Fire, 2023.

———. *Tolkien's Modern Reading: Middle-earth beyond the Middle Ages*. Washington, DC: Word on Fire, 2021.

Oxford English Dictionary. Compact ed. Oxford: Oxford University Press, 1980.

Pearce, Joseph. *Frodo's Journey*. Charlotte, NC: Saint Benedict's, 2015.

———. *Tolkien: Man and Myth, a Literary Life*. San Francisco: Ignatius, 2001.

———. "Tolkien and the Catholic Literary Revival." In *Tolkien: A Celebration*, edited by Joseph Pearce, 102–23. London: HarperCollins, 1999.

Rutledge, Fleming. *The Battle for Middle-earth: Tolkien's Divine Design in "The Lord of the Rings."* Grand Rapids: Eerdmans, 2004.

Ryken, Phillip. *Messiah Comes to Middle-earth: Images of Christ's Threefold Office in "The Lord of the Rings."* Downers Grove, IL: IVP Academic, 2017.

Shakespeare, William. "King Lear." In *William Shakespeare: The Complete Works*, edited by Stanley Wells and Gary Taylor, 943–74. Oxford: Clarendon, 1988.

———. "Macbeth." In *William Shakespeare: The Complete Works*, edited by Stanley Wells and Gary Taylor, 975–1000. Oxford: Clarendon, 1988.

Shippey, Tom. *J. R. R. Tolkien: Author of the Century*. Boston: Houghton Mifflin, 2001.

BIBLIOGRAPHY

———. *The Road to Middle-earth: How J. R. R. Tolkien Invented a New Mythology.* Boston: Houghton Mifflin, 2003.
Sibley, Brian, and John Howe. *The Maps of Tolkien's Middle-earth.* London: HarperCollins, 2003.
Sir Gawain and the Green Knight. Edited by J. R. R. Tolkien and E. V. Gordon. Rev. 2nd ed. Edited by Norman Davis. Oxford: Clarendon, 1967.
Sir Gawain and the Green Knight, Pearl, and Sir Orfeo. Edited by Christopher Tolkien. Translated by J. R. R. Tolkien. London: Allen & Unwin, 1975.
Sir Gawain and the Green Knight, Pearl, and Sir Orfeo. Edited by Christopher Tolkien. Translated by J. R. R. Tolkien. Boston: Houghton Mifflin, 2021.
Smith, Mark Eddy. *Tolkien's Ordinary Virtues: Exploring the Spiritual Themes of "The Lord of the Rings."* Downers Grove, IL: InterVarsity, 2002.
Smith, Scott L. *"The Lord of the Rings" and the Eucharist.* New Roads, LA: Holy Water, 2019.
Spirito, Guglielmo. "The Influence of Holiness: The Healing Power of Tolkien's Narrative." In *Tolkien's "The Lord of the Rings": Sources of Inspiration,* edited by Stratford Caldecott and Thomas Honegger, 199–210. Zollikffen, Switzerland: Walking Tree, 2008.
Tolkien, J. R. R. *The Adventures of Tom Bombadil.* London: HarperCollins, 2014.
———. *Beren and Luthien.* Edited by Christopher Tolkien. New York: Harper Collins, 2017.
———. *The Hobbit.* Illustrated by Alan Lee. Boston: Houghton Mifflin, 1997.
———. *The Letters of J. R. R. Tolkien: Revised and Expanded.* Edited by Humphrey Carpenter and Christopher Tolkien. London: HarperCollins, 2024.
———. *The Lord of the Rings.* 50th ann. ed. London: HarperCollins, 2005.
———. "Mythopoeia." In *Tree and Leaf,* by J. R. R. Tolkien, 83–90. London: HarperCollins, 2001.
———. "On Fairy-Stories." In *Tree and Leaf,* by J. R. R. Tolkien, 1–82. London: HarperCollins, 2001.
———. *The Silmarillion.* Edited by Christopher Tolkien. Illustrated by Ted Nasmith. Boston: Houghton Mifflin, 2004.
West, John G. "The Lord of the Rings as Defense of Western Civilization." In *Celebrating Middle-earth: "The Lord of the Rings" as a Defense of Western Civilization,* edited by John G. West, 15–30. Seattle, WA: Inkling, 2002.
Wood, Ralph C. *The Gospel According to Tolkien.* Louisville, KY: Westminster John Knox, 2003.
Zaleski, Phillip, and Carol Zaleski. *The Fellowship: The Literary Lives of the Inklings.* New York: Farrar, Strauss & Giroux, 2015.

www.ingramcontent.com/pod-product-compliance
Lightning Source LLC
Chambersburg PA
CBHW070913160426
43193CB00011B/1446